Visas

Entries/Entrées   Departures/Sorties

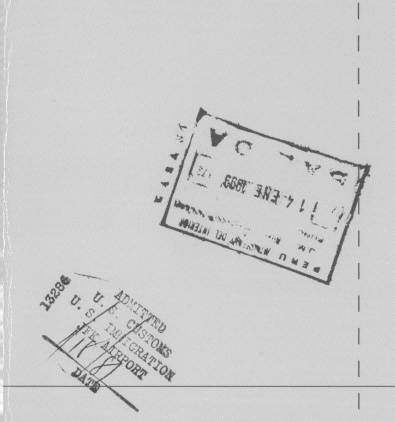

Luke & Kelsey,
Thank you so much for
planning such an amazing
evening for Jim & Dee's
anniversary. It was so
wonderful! Love, Mona

© 2016 Monika Reti.
Photography and design © 2016 Lissa Hahn.

Printed in the USA.

Hipcooks Inc., 3808 N Williams Blvd, Suite 200, Portland, Oregon 97 227.

Author's Cataloging-in-Publication data

Reti, Monika.

Hipcooks: Around the World in 12 Dinner Parties – 1st ed.

p. cm.

Includes index.

1. Cookery 2. Cookery (travel) 3. Cookery (international) I. Reti, Monika II. Title

ISBN: 978-0-615-6 9988-2

FIRST EDITION
10 9 8 7 6 5 4 3 2 1

Hipcooks

Around the world in 12 dinner parties

Eat Well
Be Well,

Monika Reti

PHOTOGRAPHY LISSA HAHN

"I am not making mudpies. . . . This is goulash."
—Monika Reti, in the sandbox, age 4

To all Hipcooks— *past, present,* **and** *future....*

To find out more about Hipcooks,
check out new recipes,
learn some tips,
or to sign up for a hands-on cooking class, visit...

www.hipcooks.com

TABLE OF CONTENTS

MONIKA'S STORY

The founder of Hipcooks, the school famous for not using recipes, is now sharing recipes of her own? Go on, poke your fun!

For me, creating this cookbook was a worldwide ticket of adventure down memory lane. With a father from Argentina, I grew up with summers of long afternoon *asados*. My dad and uncle would make a day of it, tending the fire until the coals were the perfect meat-cooking temperature. At a dining table filled with friends and family, out came course after course. If I could ask my *abuelo* in properly pronounced Spanish for *"un poco más de vino por favor,"* my little glass got filled—the perfect motivation for learning a new language.

My German mother is happiest in the kitchen or in the garden—and she creates masterpieces in each. The tenth child born into a war-torn family, she and her brothers and sisters scattered like dandelion seeds all over the globe. One sister flew to Iran, and I have a gaggle of blue-eyed Iranian cousins who love to eat almost as much as they love to laugh.

It's safe to say, I have the travel bug in me. And it is led by my palate. At age 15, I went on a solo adventure to Europe, and I've been exploring—and eating—around the world ever since.

After graduate school in England, I wandered to Venezuela, where I met a couple from Kentucky. They had spent twenty years building a sailboat in their backyard—hull, sails, and all. Never missing a chance to go exploring, I accepted an opportunity aboard and learned about the Spice Islands, picking up allspice, nutmeg, and cinnamon along the way.

My favorite part of Morocco was getting lost in the medinas. In a narrow passageway I'd be brushed by a stinky, sweaty donkey, only to turn the corner and discover, to my olfactory delight, a woman with a cartful of fresh mint for sale.

On the Greek islands, squinting in the sun and watching fishermen tenderize octopus against the seaside rocks, I realized that all you need to be happy in life is a little salt, olive oil, and lemon juice. Then, on the heels of a particularly bad breakup, I enrolled in cooking school in Thailand and learned you can heal your heart with fish sauce.

Now, "all grown up", I've found (at least for now) that traveling the globe has taken a backseat to raising my beautiful red-headed daughter. Physically, that is, since we do our globetrotting in the kitchen. Here, we let the world come to us. No passport, nor jetlag necessary.

I hope this book takes you many places and leads you to many adventures.

With love,
Monika.

THE HIPCOOKS STORY How it all got started.

Hipcooks was "founded" about ten years ago, at a dinner party (surprise, surprise!) in a Los Angeles loft.

My sister's boyfriend had just finished a lifelong dream of directing his first feature film. He wanted to celebrate with a dinner party and he needed help. His "spacious" loft was sparsely furnished – not even a dining table. And oh, he didn't cook.

My sister called me for help. The first thing I did was to take the mattress off his bed, turning the intricately carved wooden platform into a gorgeous table. Hanging silk saris from the walls and windows and scattering rose petals, candles, and pillows around the table, we transformed the spartan space into a lush and romantic setting in one afternoon.

Dinner was a blast. On the heels of a trip to Morocco, I threw together a menu spiced with cinnamon, parsley, dates, and wine. A lovely young woman walked into the kitchen. "This smells amazing! This food is fantastic! Can I help you?" Ignoring my protests for her to go enjoy the party, she insisted. "Put me to work! This looks like *fun*!" So I gave her a few quick pointers on how to use a chef's knife, and we were off.

We had a ball, even when the charming host came into the kitchen and said, "Monika, remember how I said it would be a dinner for twenty? Well, I think I have about thirty people here." On his way out he mumbled, "Um, I hope you weren't planning to use the oven. It doesn't work." That's when I turned to my new cooking partner and said, "Now the real fun begins!"

I cooked "Hipcooks-style" before Hipcooks existed, making up dishes as I went along. Smiling, laughing, and tasting along the way, we turned flavors that were ho-hum into ones that made our feet tap. A squeeze of lemon here, more garlic there, a flick of Maldon salt to top it all off.

At the end of the night, my new friend said, "I *loved* that! You have to teach me how to cook."

"But I just did! You saw how I made that dinner. You can create that again."

"Oh, no," she said. "I want to learn to cook like you. You never stressed. You never freaked out when ten more people arrived. You made food out of nothing. Teach me that."

And *Hipcooks was born.*

WELCOME TO HIPCOOKS

The recipes in this book are HIPCOOKS—STYLE, meaning that you can be as exacting or as free-form as you like while cooking. Of course we include amounts to use in our recipes, but they are just a guide. Why use measuring cups when you can use your hands instead? They say that when food is delicious, it is because the person preparing it has sweet hands.

Always taste along the way, and INSERT YOUR OWN PERSONALITY INTO THE FOOD. Have fun with the process. More spicy? Go for it! A swirl of cream? Absolutely!

Just remember, cooking is always yummiest when it comes from the heart.

TOOLS OF THE TRADE

* **A GREAT KNIFE:** A great chef is no better than her knife. Ours are Wüsthof Ikon. A honing steel keeps it sharp.

* **WOODEN CUTTING BOARD:** Knives love wood! We make beautiful round cutting boards that we sell at all our Hipcooks studios.

* **1 OR 2 GOOD POTS:** Enameled cast iron offers even heat distribution and retention. It's easy to clean. We love Le Creuset.

* **10- & 12-INCH NONSTICK SKILLETS:** We use triple-coated Vollrath for a perfect sear.

* **ENAMELED CAST-IRON CITRUS PRESS:** We have a large one, and everything fits in it—lemons, limes, and oranges. Lots of juice, no seeds!

* **VEGGIE PEELER:** U-shaped ones are best because they swivel.

* **COLANDER AND SIEVE:** For straining and dusting.

* **LARGE STAINLESS STEEL MIXING BOWLS:** For tossing, marinating, and creating a makeshift double boiler by placing one over a pot.

✳ SMALL TOOLS: Choose heat-resistant silicone tongs, spatulas, whisks, and spoons.

✳ MORTAR AND PESTLE: Because life requires freshly toasted and ground spices. A **molcajete** is perfect!

✳ ZESTER: For fine zest, a Microplane. For ribbons, a cocktail zester.

✳ FOOD PROCESSOR: Cuisinart has functionality and durability.

✳ ICE CREAM MAKER: Ours is a Cuisinart Ice-21 for sorbets and ice cream in twenty minutes.

✳ A SUPER-SMOOTH, POWERFUL BLENDER: A Vitamix will change your life — and your health!

✳ RICE COOKER: Just turn it on and forget about it!

✳ SILICONE BAKING SHEET INSERT: So that nothing sticks to your baking sheet, and clean-up is a breeze. Ours are Matfer Exopat.

✳ MEASURING CUPS AND SPOONS: Ha ha! Just kidding! This is Hipcooks; use a handful of this and a pinch of that... and trust your own judgement!

THE HIPCOOKS PANTRY

Here's what you'll find in our kitchen (and what you'll need for the recipes in this book), from the basics to the exotic. And here's what we say about substitutions: *Go for it!* Use dried rosemary if you can't find fresh, jalapeño peppers if you can't find Scotch bonnets, frozen mango when fresh is out of season. You get the idea! Omissions and additions to the recipes should be according to your likes and dislikes. *We support you!*

The Basics:

Extra virgin first cold-pressed olive oil: we use it in almost everything. So healthy for you, you can drink it straight up!

Lemons and limes: organic and unwaxed, for zesting and juicing. Feeling sassy? Add citrus!

Salt: sea salt for cooking, Maldon salt for finishing.

Fresh herbs: to make dishes pop! Parsley, sage, rosemary, and thyme. And cilantro, scallions, mint, chives, oregano, basil, and dill. How about planting a garden?

Nuts of all kinds: pine nuts, walnuts, cashews, almonds, pecans, and pistachios. Always look for the raw, unsalted kind. Store-bought almond meal is also amazing—use in place of flour, or to add a dash of richness.

Aromatics: lots of onions, garlic, and ginger are always good to have. They are the base of many dishes. Sauté any or all of these to jump-start your inner chef and get your creative juices flowing. Want to go to Mexico? Add chiles and chicken. To India? Sprinkle turmeric and coriander. To Morocco? Throw in a cinnamon stick and chopped dates.

Spice Aisle:

Allspice, whole: cute little berries from the allspice tree, they taste like cinnamon, nutmeg, and clove. Toast in a dry, hot skillet. Then grind.

Bay leaves: pick fresh from a bay tree or buy dried.

Black pepper: notice it is not omnipresent throughout this book. There is a time and a place for everything! When you choose to use it, use fresh ground.

Cardamom: buy green pods and use the black spice inside.

Cayenne pepper: buy ground, preferably in small amounts from bulk bins.

Cinnamon sticks and ground cinnamon: a naturally sweet spice that comes from the inner bark of a tree.

Cloves: buy whole cloves and use to infuse dishes. Whole cloves pack more punch than ground.

Coriander seeds: the seed pods of the cilantro plant. Toast in a dry, hot skillet. Then grind.

Cumin seeds: used in cooking throughout the globe. Toast in a dry, hot skillet. Then grind.

Filé powder: Cajun and Creole cooking use it for its distinctive flavor and thickening power.

Garam masala: a mix of warm spices. Use it as a finishing touch to Indian dishes.

Nutmeg: buy whole nutmeg and grate with a Microplane.

Saffron threads: the stamen of a type of crocus and the world's most expensive spice— but worth it.

Spanish paprika: lends a smoky depth, because it uses sweet dried chili peppers.

Star anise: buy whole, and use to infuse.

Tabasco sauce: use a sprinkle when you are feeling spicy!

Turmeric: comes from the root of a plant and tastes like a spicy carrot. It turns everything it comes into contact with sunshine yellow!

Vanilla bean paste: real vanilla bean flecks in a rich, concentrated paste. Find Nielsen-Massey brand at the Hipcooks store.

Snobby Notes:

Please buy organic whenever you can!

At Hipcooks...
- our yogurt is Greek
- our milk is organic
- our eggs are free-range
- our chocolate is dark (72% cacao)
- our butter is unsalted
- our chicken stock is organic and low- or no-sodium

Salt and pepper: are so ubiquitous, we haven't listed them in the ingredients column of each recipe. Salt should always be sea salt (Maldon to finish) and pepper should always be fresh ground!

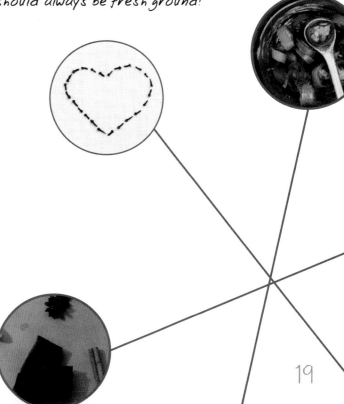

THE ETHNIC AISLE What you can't find locally, look for online!

Hispanic Market

Chorizo: look for Spanish chorizo, which is a spicy cured sausage perfect for paella.

Dried chiles: look for different kinds: ancho, mulato, pasilla, negro, and cascabel. They have subtle differences in flavor and color.

Dulce de leche: caramelized milk and sugar. Lapataia brand is outrageously yummy, but you should conduct your own scientific research to see which is best.

Hibiscus blossoms: create a tangy deep-red tea. Buy them dried, or use hibiscus tea bags in a pinch.

Valencia rice: a short, fat grain, similar to arborio rice. Cook it al dente.

Greek/Armenian/Persian Market

Barberries: Iranian red berries, called **zereshk**. If you cannot find them, you can substitute cranberries, goji berries, or even pomegranate seeds.

Halloumi: an unripened brine cheese usually made of sheep and goat's milk. It has a super-high melting point, so you can grill or fry it.

Persian cucumbers: cute little cukes known for edible skin and little seeds.

Pomegranate molasses: use it to add a tangy note to your dishes. We love it in salad dressing.

Rose water: delightful stuff. A little goes a long way.

Japanese Market

Inari skins: thin slices of tofu, pan-fried and gently sliced through the center to create a pocket, then marinated in sweet soy sauce.

Japanese cucumbers: like English cucumbers, they have an edible skin.

Matcha: a fine-ground powder from green tea.

Mirin: a rice wine condiment in Japanese cooking.

Nori: seaweed paper used for sushi-making.

Ponzu: consider using instead of soy sauce—it's lighter in color and zingier in flavor.

Thai Market

Coconut milk: Mae Ploy is our favorite because it's the creamiest.

Fish sauce: use for a pungent salty flavor. If you don't love it already, you will learn to!

Forbidden rice: also known as Thai black rice, sweet black rice, or black glutinous rice.

Fresh turmeric: is fun to use when you can find it. (It will stain, so be careful!) Otherwise, use dried.

Galangal: a spicy cousin to ginger.

Lemongrass: has a woody stalk. Use only the bottom third. When unavailable, use lemon zest or lime zest.

Lime leaves: also called kaffir lime leaves, they are rich in essential oils and impart delicious flavor. Use lime zest in a pinch.

Shiso: a purple and green leafy herb. Sometimes called Japanese mint.

Shrimp paste: fish sauce on steroids. Use it, if you dare, to give your curries a punch.

Spring roll wrappers: are usually made from rice flour, water, and salt. They are rolled out by machine to paper thinness and then dried on bamboo mats in the sun.

Thai basil: a spicy cousin to Italian basil, and great in Asian dishes.

Thai chilies: these small chilies come in red and green and are hotter than jalapeño or serrano chilies.

Thai sweet rice: look for it by name. It has a short fat grain, similar to sushi rice, but is much sweeter. To prepare, soak and then steam it.

Indian Market

Candied fennel seeds: cute and multi-colored, for a delightful breath-freshening treat.

Paneer: Indian vegetarian cheese (you can also find it at fancy grocery stores).

Papadums: flatbreads made of chickpea flour that poof when cooked.

TRAVEL OF CONTENTS

LA BELLE ÉPOQUE......82

Warm oysters with leek and Champagne sauce
Beef bourguignon
Tarte tatin with crème fraîche glacée

MY BIG FAT GREEK DINNER PARTY.....92

Sautéed halloumi with ouzo
Spanikopita
Grilled veggie salad
Rack of lamb with tzatziki
Baklava

1001 ARABIAN NIGHTS......102

Herb-studded meatballs with cucumber yogurt sauce
Chicken stewed with pomegranate and walnuts, or
Chicken with jeweled rice
Rose water and cardamom creme brulée

SHORTCUT TO NIRVANA......112

Papadums with three flavorful sauces
Saag paneer
Chicken tikka masala with fancy basmati rice
Mango, ginger, and lime sorbet

THAI ONE ON......122

Veggie spring rolls
Green curry with eggplant and mushrooms, or
Red curry with chicken and cashews
Coconut sticky rice
Forbidden rice with coconut milk

TURNING JAPANESE......132

Cucumber saketini
Inari skins with shiitake mushrooms
Himachi sashimi
Free-for-all, make-and-share sushi
Spicy tuna rolls
Matcha teacakes

RAGIN' CAJUN

Come on down to the South, y'all! We'll be fixin' and servin' up some Hipcooksified favorites with good ol' Southern hospitality.

There's no pomp and circumstance to this backyard party. The gumbo and cornbread are on the table, so grab a frosty one and just help yourself. **Laissez les bons temps rouler!**

NEW ORLEANS

MENU
CHICKEN, SHRIMP, AND ANDOUILLE SAUSAGE GUMBO

NAINAIN'S SWEET CORNBREAD

SPICY TURNIPS AND GREENS

BANANAS FOSTER WITH BUTTER PECAN ICE CREAM

serves 12

CHICKEN, SHRIMP, AND ANDOUILLE SAUSAGE GUMBO

In New Orleans, there are as many versions of gumbo as there are musicians. There's only one unifying bass line—the roux. You must respect the roux!

MARINADE

Paprika	2 teaspoons
Black pepper	1 teaspoon
Cayenne pepper	1 teaspoon
Chicken thighs	2 pounds, boneless and skinless, cut into bite-size pieces
Shrimp	1 pound, shell-on and uncooked

GUMBO

Corn oil	1/2 cup
Flour	1/2 cup
Onions	2 medium, chopped
Celery	4–5 spears, chopped
Green peppers	2 medium, chopped
Okra	1 pound, sliced and divided in half
Andouille sausage	12 ounces, thickly sliced
Filé powder	3 tablespoons, or more!
Tabasco sauce	as needed
Parsley	1 handful, chopped

SEASON THE CHICKEN: Combine the paprika, pepper, cayenne, and 2 teaspoons of salt. Rub it all over the chicken and pop in the fridge overnight.

MAKE THE SHRIMP STOCK: Peel the shrimp and set in the fridge for later. In a large pot, cover the shrimp shells with 2 quarts of water and bring to a boil. Reduce heat to simmer and cook for about 45 minutes, until flavorful. Skim any foam or impurities from the top. Remove from heat and strain.

MAKE THE ROUX: Heat the oil in a large pot (we like cast-iron) over medium-high heat. Stir in the flour and reduce the heat to medium-low. Continue stirring for 30–45 minutes until it reaches the color of peanut butter. You may need a little more oil, or a touch more flour, to get the sauce so that it coats the back of a spoon.

MAKE THE GUMBO: Stir the onions, celery, peppers (the trinity) along with half the okra into the roux. Cook 5–10 minutes, stirring often. Add the chicken, and cook another 5–10 minutes, regularly scraping the bottom of the pan. Reduce the heat if necessary to keep the roux from burning. Add the shrimp stock, stirring and scraping to make sure all of the roux is incorporated. Bring to a boil, and add the andouille. Reduce heat to low, cover, and simmer for at least an hour and a half, stirring from time to time, as you sip on a cold one.

Add the shrimp and remaining okra, and simmer for another fifteen minutes or so. Swirl in the filé powder. Taste for seasoning and add salt, cayenne, or Tabasco as needed. Top with a sprinkle of parsley.

....

✳ HIP TIP: A pound of fresh picked crab meat, stirred in after the filé powder, is a mighty fine addition to this gumbo, if you can spare the expense.

NAINAIN'S SWEET CORN BREAD

Cooked and served warm right out of the skillet, this corn bread is the perfect match for your gumbo. Any extra gets slathered with butter and eaten 'til it's gone!

Corn oil	1/2 cup, plus a little extra for the skillet
Yellow cornmeal	2½ cups
Sugar	1/4 cup
Flour	1 cup
Baking powder	3 tablespoons
Salt	2 teaspoons
Eggs	4
Whole milk	2½ cups

Preheat the oven to 400°F and oil a 10- or 12-inch cast-iron skillet (a baking pan also works fine). Warm over low heat while you make the batter. This helps set the bread and keeps it from sticking.

Combine the cornmeal, sugar, flour, baking powder, and salt. Whisk together the ½ cup oil, eggs, and milk. Stir the wet ingredients into the dry until just combined—over-mixing can result in dense cornbread. Pour the batter into the skillet (it should be about ¾ full), and bake until cooked through, about 30 minutes. Touch the center of the bread; it should spring back.

✳ **HIP TIP:** *How 'bout adding some fresh corn or chopped jalapeños to the mix? Or scatter the top with sliced scallions and grated cheese before baking, to create the prettiest thing you ever did see!*

SPICY TURNIPS AND GREENS

This classic dish gets a healthy make-over! We take a fresh and easy approach using raw collards and roasted turnips. The secret is to cut your greens super-fine.

Butter	*4 tablespoons*
Turnips	*1 pound, sliced into wedges*
Sugar	*1–2 teaspoons*
Cayenne pepper	*1/2 teaspoon*
Collard greens	*1 pound, julienned (mustard greens or kale are great, too)*
Olive oil	*1–2 tablespoons*

Preheat oven to 400°F.

Melt the butter in a skillet over medium heat, and toss in the turnips, sugar, and cayenne. Add a pinch of salt and a grind of pepper.

Spread onto a baking sheet, pop into the oven, and roast until edges are brown and tender, about 40 minutes.

While the turnips cook, massage a little salt and olive oil into the collards. When turnips are done, scatter the fresh greens over the top. Pop into a serving dish, and enjoy!

✳ **HIP TIP:** *Is this recipe too healthy for you? Well, sugar, go on ahead and add chopped uncooked bacon to your turnips when they're fixin' to go into the oven.*

BANANAS FOSTER WITH BUTTER PECAN ICE CREAM

Although this famous dish is named after a New Orleans crime-fighting commissioner, we commit our own sneaky crime by substituting white for brown sugar in the bananas. It's so much easier to caramelize!

PECANS

Pecans	1/2 pound, chopped (about 2 cups)
Butter	3 tablespoons
Sea salt	1/4 teaspoon

ICE CREAM

Brown sugar	1 cup, packed
Corn starch	2 teaspoons
Eggs	4, large
Whole milk	2 cups
Heavy cream	2 cups

BANANAS

Bananas	6, ripe but firm, peeled, halved lengthwise, and cut in half
Vanilla bean paste	2 teaspoons
Butter	6 tablespoons
White sugar	1 cup
Dark rum	1 cup

MAKE THE PECANS Toast the pecans in a dry skillet over medium-low heat until they smell marvelously nutty and begin to brown. Add 3 tablespoons of butter and the salt, tossing to coat. Cool completely.

MAKE THE ICE CREAM: Combine the brown sugar and cornstarch. Whisk in the eggs until well combined. Heat the milk and cream in a heavy pot over medium heat, until bubbles form along the edge and the mixture steams but doesn't boil. Whisk the hot milk into the eggs. Return the mixture to the pot and cook over very low heat, stirring constantly, until thick enough to coat the back of a spoon. Don't let it come to a boil, it will be thick enough well before then.

Cool the mixture completely, then churn in an ice cream maker. During the last few minutes of churning, add the pecans. Store the ice cream in an airtight container in the freezer.

MAKE THE BANANAS: Toss the bananas in the vanilla bean paste. Melt 6 tablespoons of butter in a skillet over medium heat. Stir in the sugar. Once the sugar has melted, add the bananas and stir to coat with the caramel.

Cook for 2–3 minutes until the sugar fully caramelizes and the bananas heat through. Carry to the table, add the rum, and flambé! Allow the flame to die out on its own: 1–2 minutes. Serve immediately over ice cream, spooning any pan juices on top.

⁕ **HIP TIP:** *If the sauce is very hot, the alcohol will flame on its own. If not, use a stick lighter to ignite. How big a flame you get is dependent on the amount of rum you use, so be judicious with your drama!*

JAMAICAN ME CRAZY

In the dead of winter, transport yourself to the azure waters and white sands of the Caribbean islands. Discover ripe avocado, spicy Scotch bonnet peppers, and luscious butternut squash. Allspice trees perfume the air with nutmeg, clove, and cinnamon.

Island cooking takes advantage of this indigenous bounty and more: hibiscus flowers, pineapple, coconut, and of course, rum! Stress has no place in the kitchen as these vibrant colors and flavors come together and brighten up any day.

JAMAICA

MENU

HIBISCUS TEA COCKTAIL

CARIBBEAN STEW

SHRIMP AND PAPAYA SALAD

KILLER BLACK BEAN SALAD

GRILLED JERK CHICKEN

GRILLED PINEAPPLE WITH BOOZY ICE CREAM

* serves 6

HIBISCUS TEA COCKTAIL

This is a showstopper of a cocktail. In fact, the hibiscus tea is great on its own—go on and make a double batch.

TEA

Sugar	*1 cup, plus extra for rimming the glasses*
Hibiscus blossoms	*1 cup, dried*
Ginger	*1 thumb-sized piece, peeled and grated with a Microplane*

FOR SERVING

Limes	*1–2, sliced into thin rounds*
Jamaican rum	*up to 2 ounces per serving*

MAKE THE TEA: In a large pot, bring 8 cups of water to a boil. Add the sugar and stir until dissolved. Turn off the heat, add the hibiscus and ginger, and steep for 20 minutes until the tea is the color of non-concentrated cranberry juice. Strain into a pitcher, pressing the flowers to extract all the juice. Reserve the pressed flowers for a pretty garnish. Chill.

TO SERVE: To make a beautiful sugar-rim for your cocktail, place some sugar in a shallow bowl or dish. Rub the rim of each glass with lime and dip into the sugar. Pretty! Fill the glass with ice. Add an ounce or two of rum, depending on your fortitude! Top with the tea, stir, and garnish with a lime slice and a hibiscus flower.

This drink could also be shaken in a cocktail shaker and served "straight up," with a hibiscus flower for a pretty garnish, of course!

* HIP TIP: *When spiking the tea, you may like to swap the rum with gin, vodka, or even beer. Spice up your cocktail with freshly grated nutmeg over the top—a delicious and authentic Carribean touch.*

CALLALOO: CARIBBEAN STEW

A blend of new world ingredients and African roots, callaloo is a true celebration of the West Indies. Combining indigenous elements from land and sea, this stew seems like everything but the kitchen sink has been thrown in. But once the island flavors meld, the taste is fantastically soulful.

Bacon	1/2 pound, roughly diced
Onion	1 large, diced
Garlic	5 cloves, chopped
Jalapeño peppers	2, seeded and minced (1 Scotch bonnet pepper is an authentic substitute)
Butter	1 tablespoon, as needed
Chives	1 small handful, chopped
Thyme	1 small handful (5–10 stems)
Butternut squash	1½ pounds, peeled, seeded, and cubed (about 4 cups)
Coconut milk	1 can (14 ounces)
Chicken stock	at least 2 cups
Okra	1 pound, sliced into thin rounds (buy it frozen year-round)
Kale	1 handful, roughly chopped
Spinach	1 handful, roughly chopped
Crab meat	1 can (6 ounces), drained
Tabasco sauce	for serving
Lime	for serving

In a large soup pot or stockpot, cook the bacon over medium heat, but don't drain off the fat as you normally would. Add the onion, garlic, and jalapeños and sauté until the onion is translucent. (You may need to sneak in a pat of butter if the bacon doesn't provide enough fat.) Add the chives and thyme stems, and cook till fragrant, 30–60 seconds. Stir in the squash and cook for a minute or two. Pour in the coconut milk and enough stock to cover the squash by an inch.

Reduce the heat and simmer. If you prefer a thicker stew, add the okra immediately and let it simmer with the squash. If you like the okra green and vibrant, add it in the last 3 minutes of cooking. Cook until the squash is soft, about 15 minutes. Next, add the kale and spinach, cooking until they are bright, about 3 minutes. Lastly, stir in the crab. You should have a rich, hearty stew.

Before serving, remove the thyme stems. Now, taste! You'll need to add salt and pepper for sure. Perhaps a splash of Tabasco? Serve with Tabasco and lime wedges. To make it a meal, serve with cornbread.

⁎ HIP TIP: *In Trinidad, this national dish is traditionally served on Easter Day—but you'll find that you'll be making this in any season, for any occasion!*

SHRIMP AND PAPAYA SALAD

Vanilla bean paste adds a dash of the unexpected to the delicate leaves of butter lettuce.

VANILLA CITRUS DRESSING

Olive oil	1/2 cup
Grapeseed oil	1/2 cup
Champagne vinegar	4 tablespoons (or use orange muscat vinegar)
Orange juice	from 1 orange
Lime juice	from 2 limes
Vanilla bean paste	1 ½ tablespoons
Thyme	6–8 stems, leaves removed
Scallions	6, finely sliced

SALAD

Butter leaf lettuce	2 large heads (you can also use frisée)
Ripe papaya	1, peeled, seeded, and thinly sliced (mango is a great substitute)
Avocado	1 (just-ripe), pitted, peeled, and thinly sliced
Shrimp	18, peeled, deveined, and cooked (or langostino tails)

MAKE THE SALAD DRESSING: Whisk together the oils, vinegar, orange and lime juices, vanilla bean paste, thyme, and scallions. Season with salt and pepper to your taste buds' delight.

ASSEMBLE THE SALAD: Dress the lettuce on its own, and arrange on a large platter. Next dress the papaya and avocado, and place atop the greens. Finally, dress the shrimp! Scatter all around the salad.

⁂ HIP TIP: *Take a little extra time to cut the papaya and avocado into beautiful slices, as they make the dish shine.*

KILLER BLACK BEAN SALAD

This salad is best with black beans that you've cooked yourself. Canned black beans can be too mushy. And do make this salad—it is truly fabulous!

Black beans	*2 cups dried, cooked in salted water until al dente*
Avocado	*1, peeled, pitted, and diced*
Tomatoes	*2 large, seeded and diced*
Red onion	*1 small, diced*
Corn	*1 cup cooked (fire-roasted corn from the frozen aisle is delicious!)*
Garlic	*3 cloves, finely chopped*
Cilantro	*1 handful, chopped*
Lime juice	*from 3 limes*
Olive oil	*4 tablespoons*
Maldon salt	*to finish*

Combine all the ingredients in a large bowl. Finish with a sprinkle of Maldon salt for a delightful crunch. Taste and adjust with lime juice, olive oil, and more salt, if needed.

* **HIP TIP:** *If you're bringing this salad as a side dish to a BBQ (hint hint!), save the Maldon salt for a last-minute addition. Your salad won't lose any juices, and the salt will stay crunchy.*

GRILLED JERK CHICKEN

In Jamaica, chicken is grilled over allspice wood. Mimic that flavor by adding toasted and ground allspice berries to this spicy rub.

JERK

Scallions	2 bunches, roughly chopped
Thyme	1 small handful (5–10 stems), leaves removed from stems
Sage	4 leaves
Bay leaves	3, crumbled
Ginger	1 thumb-sized piece, peeled
Whole allspice	20 berries, toasted and ground
Whole nutmeg	1/2 tablespoon or so, scraped with a Microplane
Coriander seeds	1 tablespoon, toasted and ground
Ground cinnamon	1 tablespoon
Scotch bonnet peppers	1–2, stems removed
Garlic	6 cloves
Olive oil	1/3 cup
Lime juice	from 1 lime
Chicken breasts	6–8, bone-in, skin on

MAKE THE JERK: In a food processor, whiz the scallions, thyme, sage, bay, ginger, allspice, nutmeg, coriander, cinnamon, peppers, and garlic with 2 teaspoons of salt. Inhale the freshness and give it a taste to see how the flavors are developing—if it tastes like it can handle more spice, add it! Finally, process in the oil and the lime juice. Coat the chicken with about half of the the rub, put in a covered container, and pop in the fridge for at least 3 hours or overnight. Thin the extra rub with olive oil and serve alongside the finished dish as a saucy sidekick.

GRILL THE CHICKEN: Heat the grill to medium-high.

Grill the chicken until cooked through, 5–7 minutes per side. If the weather is too chilly for grilling, you can also pan-sear the skin side of the chicken for a nice effect, then pop into a 350°F oven to finish.

⁂ HIP TIP: *Instead of chicken breasts, marinate pork loin, chicken tenders, shrimp, or any sturdy white fish like halibut or monkfish. If using seafood, marinate for a quick 30 minutes.*

GRILLED PINEAPPLE WITH BOOZY ICE CREAM

Grilled pineapple alone is spectacular, but with rum and coconut, you'll feel like you're in the West Indies no matter where you are. *Jah mahn!*

RUM SOAKED PINEAPPLE

Pineapple	1, peeled and sliced
Rum	enough to cover the pineapple (2–3 cups)
Brown sugar	1/2 cup, spread out on a plate

ICE CREAM

Milk	1 cup
Heavy cream	2 cups
Coconut milk	1 cup
Vanilla bean paste	to taste
Eggs	6 yolks, plus 2 whole
Sugar	1 cup

MAKE THE PINEAPPLE: Soak the pineapple in rum for at least 3 hours, or overnight if possible.

Drain the pineapple, reserving the delicious pineapple-flavored rum for later.

Heat grill to medium-high.

Dip each pineapple slice in brown sugar, and grill until each side is beautifully caramelized, about 3 minutes per side. Baste with the reserved rum, or drink it, saving a little to add to the ice cream—waste not, want not.

MAKE THE ICE CREAM: Scald the milk, cream, coconut milk, and vanilla bean paste. Whisk the eggs and sugar until combined. Slowly whisk the hot milk into the eggs and sugar. Return to a very low heat, stirring constantly until the custard coats the back of a spoon, about 2 minutes. Add the reserved rum (just a few tablespoons), sampling as often as necessary to be certain it's the perfect amount. Quality assurance is key.

Remove from the heat, cool completely, and churn in an ice cream maker. Once ready, spoon the mixture into a lidded container and store in the freezer.

⁂ HIP TIP: *In the dead of winter, you can still make a tropical dessert by using a kitchen torch, or your broiler, to brûlée the sugar atop the pineapple. Lighting things on fire is always in season.*

HOLY MOLE!

A lot of people think of Mexican food as quesadillas and tacos. We take it to the next level with a Mexican meal that is **auténtica**. **¡Arriba, arriba!**

A little Hipcooks twist turns the familiar into something outstanding. The margarita is made fresh in the glass; the chile relleno is baked, not fried; and the flan is spiced with pasilla chiles and is silky smooth.

And, for the star of the show: The Mole! This is a true special-occasion dish. Some versions are rumored to have over 100 ingredients with 10 different chiles. Our mole isn't quite so involved, but equally spectacular. Give yourself time to enjoy the process of making it. Play by adjusting the flavors, **poquito a poquito**. **¡Qué sabroso!**

MEXICO

MENU

IN-THE-GLASS MARGARITA

HIPCOOKS CHILE RELLENO
WITH ROASTED TOMATO SALSA

COCONUT CHICKEN IN MOLE

PASILLA CHILE FLAN

* serves 6

IN-THE-GLASS MARGARITA

MAKES 1 MARGARITA

As a true Hipcook, you *always* make your own sour mix, and in this recipe, you make it right in the glass!

SIMPLE SYRUP

Sugar	*1 cup*
Water	*1 cup*

MARGARITA

Lime juice	*from 1 lime*
Lemon juice	*from 1/2 lemon*
Orange juice	*from 1/2 orange (if desired for a sweeter flavor)*
Simple syrup	*1¼ ounces (use plain, basil, or chile infused syrup)*
Tequila	*1½ ounces, pure agave*

MAKE THE SIMPLE SYRUP: Simple syrup is easy—just boil equal parts water and sugar. But why not up the ante and infuse it as it boils with basil, chiles, or even lime zest? ¡Claro que sí!

Allow the simple syrup to cool and strain if necessary before using. Store simple syrup in your fridge; it keeps for weeks!

MAKE THE MARGARITA: Combine all of the ingredients in the pint glass of your cocktail shaker. Fill the shaker with ice. Shake!

Rim the pint glass with salt and throw in some ice. Strain the margarita on top. For a sneaky surprise, top with a splash of Champagne.

⁂ HIP TIP: *At Hipcooks, not only do we love to infuse simple syrups, but we also infuse salts! We make a chile-lime salt for margarita-glass salting. Simply grind sea salt in a food processor with your favorite additions. Mix in Maldon salt at the end, or add black lava salt for contrast of color.*

HIPCOOKS CHILE RELLENO

A very untraditional chile relleno (baked, not fried), this recipe yields a pepper that is perfectly crunchy and healthy. Of course, the cheese inside ensures it will be gooey and delicious.

Lemon zest	*from 2 lemons*
Capers	*2 teaspoons*
Parsley	*1/2 bunch, chopped*
Pasilla peppers	*6, tops cut off and seeded*
Manchego cheese	*8 ounces, cut into small chunks*

Preheat oven to 400°F.

Combine the zest, capers, and parsley. Insert a spoonful or two of the zesty filling into each pepper, along with a few chunks of manchego.

Place on a baking sheet, covering the tops with the stem end or foil. Bake for about 15 minutes until nicely charred on top (the peppers should still be fairly crunchy).

Serve, topped with roasted tomato salsa (recipe on next page).

✳ HIP TIP: *Instead of baking these chiles, you can also grill them. They're the perfect accompaniment to grilled chicken or flank steak.*

ROASTED TOMATO SALSA

These roasted tomatoes pack a huge flavor and have many uses, so make extra!

TOMATOES

Vine ripe tomatoes	6, halved and seeded
Olive oil	2–4 tablespoons
Oregano	12 stems, leaves removed (use dried if you don't have fresh)
Garlic	2 cloves, sliced
Maldon salt	

SALSA

Dried cascabel peppers	2–3, seeded (or substitute another spicy dried chile, like costeño)
Onion	1/2, chopped

ROAST THE TOMATOES: Place the tomato halves, skin side down, on a baking sheet. Drizzle with oil and sprinkle with oregano, half of the garlic, Maldon salt, and a little pepper. Roast in a 250°F oven for at least 2 hours until shrunken.

TOAST THE PEPPERS: In a well-ventilated room, toast the peppers in a dry skillet over medium heat. Press the peppers down into the pan until the skin begins to bubble, 3–4 minutes. Remove from the heat and soak in hot water for at least 30 minutes, or overnight.

MAKE THE SALSA: De-stem the cascabels, and pop in a food processor or *molcajete*. Add the onions and remaining garlic, and grind until smooth. Add the tomatoes and continue until a thick but somewhat chunky consistency is reached. Taste and adjust for salt. A swirl of olive oil imparts a rich flavor as well.

....

✳ HIP TIP: *There are endless uses for roasted tomatoes! To get your creative juices flowing, here are a few ideas: For an elegant appetizer, stuff them with ricotta cheese and sprinkle the tops with fresh mint and Maldon salt. For a delectable soup, blend with stock and fresh basil. For a heavenly pasta, toss with roasted tomatoes, goat cheese, black olives, and parsley.*

COCONUT CHICKEN IN MOLE

Revel in the satisfaction of preparing your own mole! Please give yourself time to enjoy the process—the other menu items will fall into place around this masterpiece.

NUT AND SEED PASTE

Pine nuts	1/4 cup
Almonds	1/4 cup
Pumpkin seeds	1/4 cup
Sesame seeds	1/4 cup
Coriander seeds	1 teaspoon
Cumin seeds	1 teaspoon
Garlic	2 cloves, peeled
Raisins	1/2 cup, soaked in 1/2 cup boiling water for 20 minutes

CHILE PASTE

Dried Mexican chiles	3–4 (a combo of anchos, mulatos, and pasillas)

MOLE BASE

Onions	2, quartered
Garlic	2 cloves
Tomatillos	4, quartered
Tomatoes	4, quartered
Serrano or jalapeño pepper	1, halved and seeded
Olive oil	1–2 tablespoons
Star anise	2–3 pods
Cinnamon	2–3 sticks
White wine	1 cup
Chicken stock	1–2 cups (as needed)
Dark chocolate	1/3–1/2 pound (70% cacao or higher)

COCONUT CHICKEN

Chicken thighs	6, bone-in and skinless
Dried unsweetened coconut	1 cup
Butter	2 tablespoons
Cooked rice	6 cups, still warm

MAKE THE NUT AND SEED PASTE: In a sauté pan over medium-low heat, combine the pine nuts, almonds, pumpkin seeds, sesame seeds, coriander, and cumin. Toast until the nuts are brown and fragrant. Process in a food processor with the garlic. Add the raisins, strained of their soaking liquid, and continue to process. You'll get a fine paste. Add some of the raisin soaking liquid if needed. Taste, and try not to eat it all. Spoon the nut and seed paste into a bowl—don't bother washing out the food processor.

MAKE THE CHILE PASTE: In a well-ventilated room, toast the dried chiles on both sides in a dry skillet over medium heat. Press the chiles into the pan until the skins begin to bubble, 3–4 minutes. Turn off the heat, cover the chiles in boiling water, and soak for a minimum of 30 minutes, up to overnight. Drain the chiles, reserving their soaking liquid. Remove the stems from the rehydrated chiles, and pop into the food processor. Process into a dark paste. Add a little of the chile soaking liquid as needed. Transfer to a bowl and don't clean the food processor just yet, Speedy Gonzales!

ASSEMBLE THE MOLE: Pop the onions, garlic, tomatillos, tomatoes, and serrano into the food processor. Pulse a few times until the veggies are chopped. Heat a swirl of olive oil in a sauté pan over medium-high heat. Sauté the chopped veggies until softened, about 5 minutes. Stir in the star anise, cinnamon, and wine. Let the wine reduce by half, then remove the whole spices.

Now it's time to play! Continue cooking the mole as you stir in a few spoonfuls of the nut and seed paste and the chile paste. Taste to see how the flavors develop. Depending on your taste buds, you may want to add the full amount of both pastes, or use less of one or the other. If your pan becomes a little dry, add some of the chile soaking liquid (for a spicier flavor) or chicken stock (for a deep, rich flavor), or both! Naturally, it will need a sprinkling of sea salt.

Now you'll need to decide whether you want your mole absolutely smooth, or a bit chunky. If you like it smooth, return the whole kit and kaboodle back to the food processor, and process again (your hardworking machine is ready to wash!).

When your mole is just right, remove from the heat and grate in the chocolate, so that it melts instantly. This will give the mole a deep, dark flavor. Holy Mole!

COOK THE CHICKEN: Preheat the oven to 375°F. Dredge the chicken in the coconut. Melt the butter in an oven-safe pan over medium-high heat, and brown the chicken on both sides. Pop the pan into the oven until cooked through, about 20 minutes. Remove from the oven, and let rest for 5 minutes. Serve with the mole and rice.

※ HIP TIP: Mole is a delightful accompaniment to roast turkey—why not mole-fy your next Thanksgiving? Or smother a whole side of fish, such as monkfish or turbot, in mole. Bake in a hot oven, and the mole becomes a fragrant crust!

PASILLA CHILE FLAN

This flan is a must-make! It uses no gelatin and has the perfect proportion of milk and cream to yield a smooth, creamy custard.

CARAMEL

Sugar	1 cup

CUSTARD

Heavy cream	1 cup
Whole milk	1/2 cup
Pasilla pepper	1 seeded, and finely chopped
Eggs	2 whole, plus 1 extra yolk
Brown sugar	1/3 cup
Vanilla bean paste	1–2 teaspoons
Orange zest	from 1 orange

Preheat oven to 350°F.

Arrange six (6-ounce) cups on a baking sheet. You can use ramekins, custard cups, or even teacups.

MAKE THE CARAMEL: In a saucepan, melt the sugar over medium-high heat. There's no need to stir until just after the first plume of steam appears. Continue stirring slowly as the caramel forms—the sugar will melt completely and turn caramel-colored. Remove the pan from the heat.

At this point, you can have fun making caramel designs! Allow the caramel to cool slightly, so that when poured from the spoon, it falls in a thick, steady stream. Make six curlicue designs on top of a silicone pan liner (like a Silpat or Exopat). When the caramel designs cool, they'll easily lift off the silicone.

You'll need the remaining caramel for the bottom of the flan cups. But first, stir in 1/2 cup of water into the caramel to make it less viscous. Heat again, if necessary, so that the water dissolves completely into the caramel. Spoon the caramel into your cups.

MAKE THE CUSTARD: Combine the cream, milk, and pasilla over medium-low heat. Cook until bubbles form, and stir. Taste to make sure the chiles have imparted their flavor to your satisfaction. Strain to remove the peppers. In a separate bowl, combine the eggs and brown sugar with a few beats of a whisk, and then add the cream mixture. Stir in the vanilla bean paste and zest, and taste. Adjust as necessary, and add the custard to your cups.

Fill the baking sheet with a half inch of water, and bake until the liquid on top of the custards is just set—they will jiggle a little when shaken—about 30 minutes. Cool in the fridge for at least 2 hours, up to overnight.

To serve, run a small knife around the flan to loosen. Place a plate over the cup and flip. Gently shake to release the flan, allowing the caramel syrup to run over.

✳ HIP TIP: Why stop at pasilla chile flan? You can also use dried anchos or mulatos to infuse flavor. Other sexy additions include a dash of grated dark chocolate and a splash of brandy. A sprinkling of Maldon salt on top will take it to a new level!

THE THRILL OF THE GRILL

Prepare this menu as a casual backyard dinner, Argentine-style. Fire up the grill and savor a meal as bright and flavorful as summer itself. It's a snap!

Light a few candles, throw some wildflowers in a jam jar, and the outdoor table is set. When your guests arrive, a chilled glass of clerico—Argentina's national summertime drink—awaits. Since you've already prepared the zucchini parcels, chimichurri, and the dessert a day in advance, all you need to do is grill the steaks and enjoy the pleasant company of your guests.

Serve dinner with an Argentine Malbec, **por supuesto!**

ARGENTINA

MENU

WHITE SANGRIA

ZUCCHINI PARCELS STUFFED WITH MUSHROOMS

GRILLED STEAKS WITH CHIMICHURRI

DULCE DE LECHE MOUSSE

* serves 6

CLERICO: WHITE SANGRIA

Light and refreshing, clerico is served on hot summer days in Argentina—in gardens, by the seaside, at outdoor cafés—any place good for sipping and people-watching.

White wine	*1 (750 ml) bottle, chilled (inexpensive white wine is just fine!)*
Orange	*1, thinly sliced*
Lime	*1/2, thinly sliced*
Mango-passion fruit juice	*1/2 quart (peach juice is a great substitute)*
Orange liqueur	*1/4 cup (Citronge, Grand Marnier, or Cointreau)*

ANY OF THE FOLLOWING FRUIT

Apples	*1, cored and sliced*
Nectarines	*1, pitted and sliced*
Green grapes	*1/2 cup, removed from stem and sliced in half*
Plums	*1, pitted and sliced*
Strawberries	*1 cup, hulled and quartered*

Combine the wine, orange and lime slices, juice, and orange liqueur in a pretty pitcher. Muddle with a long spoon. Stir in the rest of your fruit and refrigerate. Make this up to 8 hours in advance, but no more than a day before—unless you have plans for conquest. The fruit will continue to ferment, making the drink quite potent!

Serve in chilled glasses with ice.

. . . .

✳ HIP TIP: *So your guests can linger over the clerico, serve with a plate of artisanal cheeses and charcuterie.*

ZUCCHINI PARCELS STUFFED WITH MUSHROOMS

A very elegant dish that is easy to prepare. You can also make these bite-sized to serve as an appetizer.

FILLING

Garlic	4 cloves, minced
Olive oil	1–2 tablespoons, plus a little extra for garnish
Portobello mushrooms	3/4 pound, roughly chopped
Lemon	1, zested with a cocktail zester and halved
Basil	1 bunch, sliced (or use mint or parsley), saving some for garnish

PARCELS

Zucchini	3 (you want the largest you can find)
Pine nuts	1/4 cup, toasted
Maldon salt	to finish

MAKE THE FILLING: Sauté the garlic in a swirl of olive oil over medium-high heat until just sizzling. Add the mushrooms and cook until they are barely soft. Squeeze in half of the lemon and continue cooking until the mushrooms are tender. Remove from heat, add a healthy pinch of salt, and toss in most of the basil.

GRILL THE ZUCCHINI: Slice the zucchini lengthwise as thinly as possible—a sharp knife or mandolin are both great tools for this task. Brush the slices with oil and cook on a hot grill (or grill pan) until charred and soft, a few minutes on each side. Cool.

ASSEMBLE THE PARCELS: Lay two pieces of zucchini side by side, overlapping slightly lengthwise. Repeat with another two pieces and lay them atop your original slices so they make an **X**. Place a spoonful of filling in the center. Fold the parcel together by wrapping the bottommost zucchini slices up and over the filling, then fold in the upper slices. Place on a serving plate, seal side down, and repeat with remaining zucchini and filling.

GARNISH THE PARCELS: Sprinkle liberally with toasted pine nuts, lemon curls, the remaining basil, a few splashes of olive oil, and a dash of Maldon salt. Even an Argentine would be impressed!

Covered, these keep beautifully at room temperature up to several hours, or in the fridge for several days.

✳ **HIP TIP:** *If you don't already own them, treat yourself to a cocktail zester and a Microplane— they will change your life!*

GRILLED STEAKS WITH CHIMICHURRI

Traditional chimichurri uses dried herbs and spices with no lemon, but at Hipcooks we couldn't resist a very fresh and sassy version to land atop these juicy steaks.

CHIMICHURRI

Garlic	5 cloves, chopped
Parsley	1 bunch, leaves removed from stems and finely chopped
Oregano	1/2 bunch (6–10 sprigs), finely chopped
Jalapeño pepper	1/2, seeded and finely diced (red chile flakes are a great substitute)
Lemons	2, zested and juiced
Sea salt	1/2 teaspoon
Olive oil	1/2 cup, plus a little extra for grilling
Steaks	6 (4-ounce) steaks, such as top sirloin, rib eye, or filet mignon

MAKE THE CHIMICHURRI: Combine the garlic, parsley, oregano, jalapeño, lemon zest and juice, and sea salt. Stir in enough olive oil to create a perfectly drippy sauce. Taste, tap your toes, and adjust as needed.

GRILL THE STEAKS: Remove the steaks from the fridge 30 minutes before grilling.

Heat the grill to medium-high.

Brush the steaks with a bit of olive oil. Grill on both sides until cooked to your preference. At Hipcooks, we prefer to season the steaks with Maldon salt after they come off the grill.

Rest the meat for a few minutes and serve with the chimichurri.

* **HIP TIP:** *How do you like your steak? Instead of cutting into the meat to check for doneness, try this age-old chef trick: Touch your thumb to your middle finger and with your other index finger, poke the fleshy part of your thumb. Rare! Rare meat feels just that soft when you poke it. Next, touch your thumb to your ring finger (medium), and then pinky finger (well done). You'll have perfectly cooked steaks without losing any of the juices—just give them a good poke!*

DULCE DE LECHE MOUSSE

If the boozy fruit from the clerico isn't dessert enough, try this light and airy mousse as a finishing touch.

Heavy cream	*2 cups*
Dulce de leche	*1 cup (Lapataia brand is my sister's personal favorite, after conducting significant research and several blindfolded trials. It has the smoothest consistency and the best flavor.)*
Dark chocolate	*for garnish*

Whip the cream until stiff—reserve about a cup of plain whipped cream for later. Add the dulce de leche to the remaining cream and beat again until soft peaks form.

Evenly distribute half of the dulce de leche mixture into six of the prettiest glasses you can find. Layer with a dollop of the reserved whipped cream. Top with the remaining dulce de leche mixture and chill for at least 2 hours.

Upon serving, top with shaved chocolate.

....

HIP TIP: Dulce de leche is a staple in Argentina and Uruguay and enjoyed in so many ways: folded into crêpes, with bananas, in coffee, or—our favorite—straight out of the jar with a spoon.

A NIGHT IN CASABLANCA

This menu, an exotic mix of sweet and savory, is typical of what you'll find in a Moroccan medina—its labyrinthine souk a feast for the senses. Envision overflowing mounds of colorful and fragrant spices, rich carpets and bright pottery. Hear the distant call to prayer.

So that you can delight in setting up for dinner, get most of your cooking done the day before. Throw some rich fabric over your table, hang Moroccan-style lanterns, and arrange some candles for lighting. As a finishing touch, strew rose petals on your table or walkway. Sit back with the casual elegance of a Moroccan, inhale the perfume wafting from your kitchen, and enjoy.

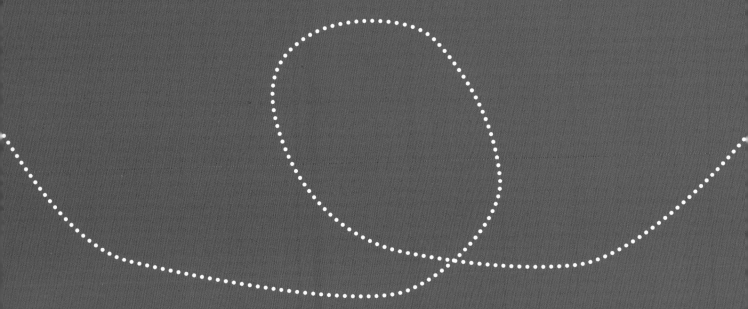

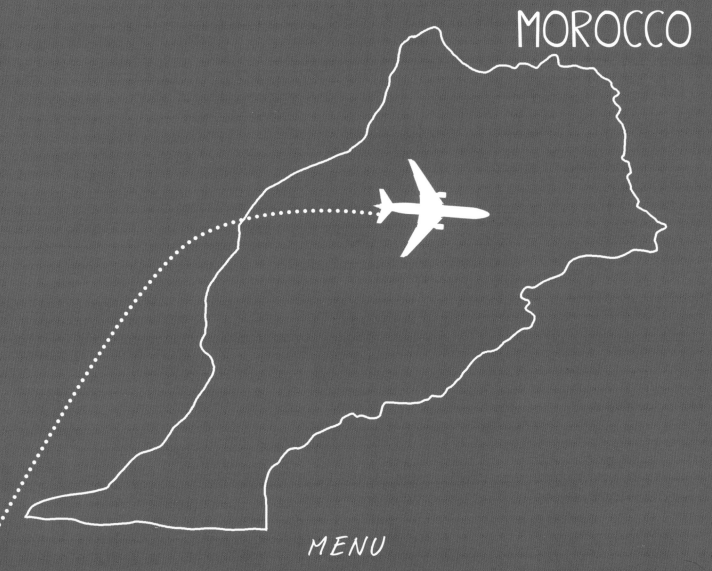

MOROCCO

MENU

B'STILLA WITH PARSLEY SALAD

CHICKEN TAGINE WITH MELTING ONIONS, PRESERVED LEMON, AND OLIVES

POACHED APRICOTS STUFFED WITH MASCARPONE

✳ serves 6

B'STILLA: MOROCCAN PASTRY WITH CINNAMON, DATES, AND PINE NUTS

At Hipcooks we make mini-b'stillas, rather than the traditional large pie, for easy serving and eating. These sweet-and-savory flaky pastries are a showstopper!

FILLING

Olive oil	1–2 tablespoons
Onion	1 large, diced
Garlic	1 clove, chopped
Ground lamb	1 pound (you can also use ground beef, or a 50/50 mix)
Cinnamon	1/2 teaspoon, plus more for dusting
Allspice	1/2 teaspoon
Pine nuts	1/3 cup, toasted
Dates	1/3 cup, chopped (currants, raisins, or apricots also work)
Parsley	1 handful, chopped

PASTRY

Phyllo	12 sheets
Butter	6 tablespoons, melted
Powdered sugar	enough for dusting (about 1 teaspoon)

MAKE THE FILLING: Heat a swirl of olive oil in a pan over medium-high heat. Add the onions and sauté until translucent. Stir in the garlic and cook until fragrant, about 30 seconds. Add the lamb, cinnamon, and allspice, breaking apart any large lumps of meat with a spatula. When the meat is just barely cooked, remove from the heat and stir in the pine nuts, dates, and parsley. Add salt and pepper to taste. Allow to cool before assembly.

ASSEMBLE THE PASTRIES: Lay a single sheet of phyllo on a flat surface. Brush the sheet with melted butter. Fold in half, lengthwise, and then again. Place a heaping spoonful of filling near the right corner. Fold the corner up and over the filling so that it makes a triangle. Continue folding the triangle to the end of the sheet, so that all the edges are completely sealed (see step-by-step photographs to the right). Don't worry if the phyllo tears occasionally. Repeat with the remaining phyllo and filling. Brush the tops of the pastries with a little more butter. These can be refrigerated or frozen to bake later.

When you're ready to bake the pastries, preheat oven to 375°F.

Bake until crispy and golden, about 20 minutes. Allow to cool for a minute, then transfer to a serving platter. Sprinkle with powdered sugar and cinnamon and serve. Flakiness guaranteed!

✳ **HIP TIP:** *Make life easy on yourself and make the b'stillas days before your dinner party. Freeze on a baking tray, then transfer to a freezer bag. When ready to bake, brush with melted butter and throw into a hot oven—no need to defrost! They'll just take a minute or two longer to bake.*

PARSLEY SALAD

If you've never had a salad of just parsley leaves, you're in for a real treat—trust us! The palate-cleansing attributes of the parsley pair beautifully with the rich flavors of the b'stilla.

Italian parsley	*2 bunches, leaves only—pinch off the stem (curly parsley also works)*
Lemon juice	*from 1 lemon*
Olive oil	*to taste*
Maldon salt	*to taste*

Combine all of the ingredients and serve! You and your guests will be making parsley salad for years to come!

✳ HIP TIP: *The only dressing you really need for any salad is a hearty squeeze of lemon, a swirl of olive oil, and a dash of Maldon salt. In fact, those three magic ingredients are pretty much all you need in life.*

PRESERVING LEMONS

You'll need preserved lemons for the chicken tagine recipe that follows, and instead of buying them you should experience the joy of making your own.

Lemons	*4, organic and unwaxed (try Meyer lemons when in season!)*
Coarse sea salt	*1/2 cup*
Granulated sugar	*1/2 cup*

Wash the lemons, and slice into thin rounds. Using your hands, massage the salt and sugar into the lemons, making sure they are well incorporated. Transfer to a glass container with a tight-fitting lid. Set aside on your counter for a couple of weeks, turning the container upside down every few days, so that all lemons get equal preserving opportunities. They look gorgeous, and will beckon you to plan your next Moroccan feast.

The lemons are ready when the skins are tender and tasty. Before you use them, you may want to rinse them to remove excess brine. Depending on their use, you can leave the slices whole or chop them.

✳ **HIP TIP:** *Oh, consider the possibilities of beautiful jars of preserved lemons! They make great gifts and are delicious with meat and fish. How about a preserved lemon slice in your gin and tonic? Now you speak our language!*

CHICKEN TAGINE WITH MELTING ONIONS, PRESERVED LEMON, AND OLIVES

A very classic Moroccan dish. This recipe is also divine with fish instead of chicken.

MARINADE

Preserved lemon	1/4 cup, rinsed and roughly chopped (see page 69)
Garlic	6 cloves, roughly chopped
Ground ginger	1 teaspoon
Cumin seeds	1/2 teaspoon, freshly toasted and ground
Paprika	1/2 teaspoon
Cayenne pepper	1/2 teaspoon
Chicken thighs	6, bone-in and skinless

TAGINE

Olive oil	1–2 tablespoons
Onions	3, halved and sliced into half-moons
Ground turmeric	1/2 teaspoon
Chicken stock	3 cups, at least
Saffron threads	1/2 teaspoon
Green olives	1/4–1/2 cup, pitted and slightly smashed
Cilantro	1 handful, chopped
Couscous	6 cups cooked, still warm (we also love Israeli couscous)

MAKE THE MARINADE: Combine the preserved lemon, garlic, ginger, cumin, paprika, and cayenne. Rub it all over the chicken. Place in a covered container and put it in the fridge—a day in advance is perfect, but a minimum of three hours will do.

Preheat oven to 275°F.

MAKE THE TAGINE: Heat a swirl of olive oil in a big, shallow pan over medium heat. Add the onions and sauté. As they soften, stir in the turmeric—all will turn delightfully yellow. Stir in the stock and the saffron. When the stock begins to simmer, remove from the heat and pour into a shallow baking dish. Nestle the chicken on top. Add enough stock to almost cover the chicken.

Transfer the dish to the oven, and cook for 90 minutes. Remove from the oven, turn the chicken, and add the olives. Return the pan to the oven for another 30 minutes, until the chicken is completely cooked and beginning to brown. Taste the sauce. It should taste a bit salty from the lemons, oil, and olives—add salt and pepper only if you need to.

This dish lends itself well to being made in advance and then gently heated before serving.

When you're ready to serve, mix a cup or so of pan juices into the couscous. Scatter cilantro over the chicken stew. Serve the couscous alongside the chicken stew.

* HIP TIP: *Couscous is the traditional pairing for this dish, and couldn't be easier. 1 to 1 is the magic ratio of liquid to couscous, but don't just use boiling water. The golden pan juices from the chicken impart an exotic flavor!*

POACHED APRICOTS STUFFED WITH MASCARPONE

At Hipcooks, we love to bring three bowls to the table—one with the apricots, one with the mascarpone, and one with pistachios. Guests can lazily assemble dessert for one another, while lingering over wine and good conversation!

SYRUP

Sugar	*1 ¼ cups*
Vanilla bean paste	*1 teaspoon*
Lemon juice	*1 tablespoon*
Dried apricots	*18, soaked in water overnight and drained*

FILLING

Mascarpone	*1 cup, at room temperature*
Vanilla bean paste	*1 teaspoon*
Powdered sugar	*1 teaspoon*
Lemon zest	*from one lemon*

FOR DIPPING

Pistachios	*3 tablespoons, finely chopped*

MAKE THE SYRUP: Combine the sugar, vanilla bean paste, and lemon juice with 1 ¼ cups of water in a saucepan over medium-high heat. Boil until the sugar dissolves. Reduce heat, add the apricots, and simmer for 20 minutes, or until the apricots are divinely soft and the syrup coats the back of a spoon. Cool completely. Reserve extra syrup for serving, or to sweeten tea.

SWEETEN THE MASCARPONE: Stir together the mascarpone, vanilla bean paste, powdered sugar, and zest until smooth. Taste, and adjust flavorings to your liking.

ASSEMBLE THE APRICOTS: Have your guests fill their apricots with the mascarpone mixture. Seal by running the open end of the apricots through the pistachios.

....

✳ *HIP TIP: If you'd like to prepare these in advance, fill a pastry bag with the sweetened mascarpone—it'll make filling the apricots a snap!*

¡VIVA ESPAÑA!

The only possible menu choice to represent Spain has to be their national dish: paella. It's as diverse as Spain's distinct regions: rabbit and chorizo for the interior, mariscos for the coastline.

Lucky you! Because paella is so versatile, it can be served straight out of the pan in a variety of settings—on your dining room table, at your kitchen counter, off the grill, or even outside in the park. No matter where they eat it, your guests will stamp their feet and clap their hands. ¡Olé!

SPAIN

MENU
SEARED SQUID OVER BRUSCHETTA
PAELLA
RED WINE SOAKED CITRUS

✳ serves 6

SEARED SQUID OVER BRUSCHETTA

Marinated squid cooked in a fast sear is so tender and flavorful—even the squid-squeamish will lick their fingers and say ¡Más, por favor!

MARINADE

Squid	1 pound, tubes and tentacles, cleaned (it's usually sold that way)
Garlic	2–3 cloves, chopped, plus 2 cloves left whole
Jalapeño pepper	1, seeded and finely diced
Lemon zest	from 1 lemon
Parsley	1 small bunch, chopped, reserving a few tablespoons for garnish

SALAD

Olive oil	1–2 tablespoons
Tomatoes	2, seeded and roughly chopped
Capers	1/4 cup
Kalamata olives	1/4 cup, pitted and chopped
Lemon juice	from 1 lemon
Maldon salt	to finish

BRUSCHETTA

Ciabatta bread	6 slices, toasted

MAKE THE MARINADE: Cut the squid tubes in half lengthwise, running your knife along the inside to remove any remaining cartilage or particles. Slice into strips about 2 inches in length. Rinse and pat dry. Combine the squid tubes and tentacles, chopped garlic, jalapeño, zest, and parsley, stirring evenly to coat. Pop in the fridge for at least 3 hours, up to overnight.

COOK THE SQUID: Heat a swirl of olive oil in a sauté pan over high. Sear the squid on both sides until just cooked, 1–2 minutes (it will be opaque throughout). Add the tomatoes, capers, olives, and lemon juice. Toss to combine, and immediately turn off the heat. Taste, and finish with a sprinkle of Maldon salt and reserved parsley.

ASSEMBLE THE TOASTS: If you rub whole garlic cloves on ciabatta toasts, they will be *fantástico!* Trump yourself and dunk the top side of each toast in the pan juices. Top with the squid, and serve.

⚹ **HIP TIP:** *Bruschetta is a favorite at Hipcooks. Top with fresh fig, prosciutto, and goat cheese. Or roasted peppers and basil. Gorgonzola and grilled peaches. Roasted tomato and ricotta. Picking up what we're putting down? Even the simplest version, drizzled with olive oil and rubbed with garlic and a ripe tomato, is* **fabuloso**. *Best eaten over the kitchen sink.*

PAELLA

This recipe ensures a robust, flavorful rice that develops the famous *socarrat* on the bottom. No matter what protein you choose to put in the paella, the star of this dish is always the rice itself.

Chicken stock	3–4 cups, as needed
Saffron	2 teaspoons

SOFRITO

Olive oil	2–3 tablespoons
Onion	1 small, finely chopped
Garlic	3–4 cloves, finely chopped
Red pepper	1, finely chopped
Green pepper	1, finely chopped
Tomatoes	3, seeded and finely chopped or grated
Spanish paprika	1/4 teaspoon (smoked or sweet)
Cayenne pepper	1/4 teaspoon

FOR THE PROTEIN, MIX AND MATCH: CHOOSE ANY THAT YOU LIKE FROM THE BELOW

Chicken tenders	1 pound
Spanish chorizo	1/2 pound (spicy dry), casings removed and sliced
Mussels	1/2 pound
Clams	1/2 pound
Shrimp	1/2 pound
Squid	1/2 pound
Cod	1/2 pound (monkfish is also great)

RICE

Valencia rice	2½ cups (Arborio rice is also great)
Edamame	1/2 cup, shelled
Maldon salt	to finish
Lemons	1–2, sliced into wedges
Parsley	1 small bunch, chopped

BLOOM THE SAFFRON: Heat 2 cups of chicken stock until just simmering. Remove from the heat, and stir in the saffron.

MAKE THE SOFRITO: In a sauté or paella pan, heat a generous swirl or two of olive oil over medium heat. Stir in the onion, garlic, red and green peppers, and tomatoes. Cook until the veggies are soft and jammy, 15–20 minutes. Stir in the paprika and cayenne.

If you are using them, now is the time to add the chicken and the chorizo. Cook for another minute. If you are omitting these ingredients, just move along to the next step.

MAKE THE RICE: Add the rice to the veggies, stirring continuously until the rice has absorbed all the liquid in the pan. Once the pan is dry, add the saffron and stock, plus enough extra stock to cover the rice by about half an inch. Stir gently to blend. Now stop stirring—good heavens, you don't want to force the starch from the rice, or prevent the crispy bottom layer *(the socarrat)* from forming!

Reduce the heat to low and simmer until all the liquid has been absorbed and the rice is just before al dente, 15–20 minutes. Stir gently and taste for doneness and flavor. You can add liquid a little at a time until the rice is just right—it should be slightly crunchy in the back of the jaw.

If you're using seafood, nestle it into the rice in a pretty fashion. Top with the edamame. Cover the pan with foil and cook for another minute or two to steam the seafood and open the shellfish.

Turn off the heat and let it rest for 10 minutes, until the rice is perfectly cooked. The crust will continue to form on the bottom of the pan as it sits.

FINISH THE PAELLA: Taste! Add a sprinkle of Maldon salt and a squeeze of lemon. Toss parsley over the top, garnish with extra lemon slices, and serve.

HIP TIP: *Paella is a veritable one-dish wonder. You can cook it in the oven, or over an open flame, or even on your grill outside! Cook it in a giant dish, and guests can help themselves to it all evening long. ¡Olé!*

RED WINE SOAKED CITRUS

This classic Spanish dessert is perfectly refreshing after a full meal.

FOR THE SYRUP

Inexpensive red wine	1 (750-ml) bottle (Charles Shaw works a charm)
Sugar	1 cup
Cinnamon	2 sticks

ANY CITRUS FROM BELOW (ABOUT 2 POUNDS TOTAL)

Oranges
Clementines
Blood oranges
Pink grapefruit

Bring the wine, sugar, and cinnamon sticks to a boil in a saucepan, stirring until the sugar dissolves. Boil until the mixture reduces to 1½ cups. Remove cinnamon sticks and cool the liquid completely—it becomes syrupy as it cools.

Remove the peel and white pith from all of the citrus with a sharp knife. Slice the citrus into pretty rounds and cover with the syrup. Chill. This, like you, improves with age. Feel free to make in advance, up to several days.

....

✗ HIP TIP: What to do with all that lovely citrus peel? Of course, you can use it to infuse simple syrup (see page 46). But why stop there? Once the syrup is infused, remove the peels, sprinkle with more granulated sugar, and dry them in a very low-heat oven or dehydrator. These crunchy peels make a tangy snack, and are perfect served alongside espresso.

LA BELLE ÉPOQUE

Decant your wine, pop in "**La vie en rose**," and let the steam on your windows beckon your guests to this refined but unpretentious meal. **Ooh la la**—you've created a warm French bistro at home.

Beef bourguignon is a classic menu choice. The Hipcooks version is easy—pop it in the oven and forget about it. Even better, you can feed a crowd inexpensively, without forgoing elegance and style.

With so much richness for the main course, you'll want to supply your guests with lighter fare on either side. Briny oysters sparkle on the tongue to start, while the sweet tarte and tangy glacée round out the evening.

FRANCE

MENU

WARM OYSTERS WITH LEEK AND CHAMPAGNE SAUCE

BEEF BOURGUIGNON

TARTE TATIN WITH CRÈME FRAÎCHE GLACÉE

*serves 6

WARM OYSTERS
WITH LEEK AND CHAMPAGNE SAUCE

Of course, raw oysters on the half-shell are divine. This recipe warms the oysters ever so slightly in a creamy sauce—perfect for slurping!

Fresh shucked oysters	*24, reserving shells and juices*

SAUCE

Leek	*1, trimmed of roots and dark green tops*
Butter	*2 tablespoons*
Champagne	*1 cup (substitute white wine if need be)*
Cream	*1/2 cup*
Chervil	*Chopped for garnish (parsley is a fine substitute)*

Have your local fish market shuck the oysters if you don't want to shuck them yourself. Store in the fridge until ready to use.

Cut the leek lengthwise down the middle and thinly slice. Wash the slices free of any grit.

Melt the butter in a saucepan over medium heat. Add the leeks and champagne. Cook until the liquid has reduced and the leeks are soft. Stir in the cream and cook until thickened, 1–2 minutes. Remove from the heat. Add the oysters and their juices, and swirl the pan to combine. Taste, and adjust with salt and pepper.

Spoon one oyster into each half-shell, cover with extra sauce, and top with chervil. Serve immediately.

* **HIP TIP:** *A fun cocktail to make with the leftover Champagne is Ernest Hemingway's "Death in the Afternoon." His original instructions said, "Pour one jigger absinthe into a Champagne glass. Add iced Champagne until it attains the proper opalescent milkiness. Drink three to five of these slowly." At Hipcooks, we add a splash of pastis or Pernod instead of absinthe, which can be tricky to find.*

BEEF BOURGUIGNON

Since this dish improves with age, pour yourself a glass of Burgundy, put on your best French accent, and enjoy a slow-paced afternoon in your aromatic kitchen, the day before your dinner party.

MARINADE

Carrots	4, diced
Celery spears	3, diced
Onion	1 large, diced
Garlic	6 cloves, chopped
Beef stew meat	3 pounds, cut into 1½-inch cubes, extra fat removed
Red wine	1 bottle
Whole cloves	2–3
Cinnamon	1 stick

STEW

Flour	1/3 cup
Bacon	1/2 pound, chopped
Olive oil	1–2 teaspoons, as needed
Cognac	1/2 cup
Tomato paste	1 heaping tablespoon
Beef stock	2–3 cups, as needed

BOUQUET GARNIS

Thyme	6 sprigs
Bay leaves	2
Sage leaves	4
Parsley	6 sprigs

FINISHING TOUCHES

Bacon	1/2 pound, chopped
Fresh pearl onions	1 cup, peeled and halved if large
Cognac	1/2 cup
Brown sugar	1/4 cup
Butter	1 tablespoon
Cremini mushrooms	1/2 pound, quartered (about 2 cups)
Dark chocolate	1–2 ounces (70% cacao or higher), finely chopped

FOR SERVING, YOUR CHOICE OF...

Buttered noodles
French bread
or herbed potatoes

MAKE THE MARINADE: Combine the *mirepoix*—carrots, celery, and onions—with the garlic and beef. Transfer to a container with a lid. Cover with wine, add the cloves and cinnamon, and refrigerate for at least 8 hours, or overnight.

MAKE THE STEW: Preheat oven to 275°F. Remove the meat from the marinade and drain (reserve wine and veggies for later). Season the flour with 1 tablespoon of salt and a teaspoon of black pepper. Pat the meat dry, and lightly coat in flour, discarding any excess.

Cook ½ pound of the bacon in a large sauté pan over medium-high heat, until the fat has rendered and the bacon is crisp. Remove from the pan and set aside. Don't clean out the pan. Add the beef to the pan and cook until brown on all sides, adding olive oil if necessary. (Do this in batches if your pan isn't large enough to accommodate all the beef in one layer.) Set aside with the bacon. Add the cognac to deglaze the pan, scraping up any brown bits with a spoon. Extra points for flambé! Strain the wine from the veggies, remove the cloves and cinnamon stick, and add the veggies to the pan. Once they are soft and fragrant, thoroughly stir in the tomato paste. Cover with the wine, and cook for several minutes. Remove from the heat and transfer to a braising pan. Add the beef and bacon. Using kitchen twine, tie together the herbs for the bouquet garnis, and add to the pot. Add enough stock to cover everything nicely. Cover the pot, and pop in the oven for 3 hours, until the meat is very tender.

FINISHING TOUCHES: In a sauté pan over high heat, cook the remaining bacon and pearl onions together until browned. When the pan is dry, deglaze once again with cognac. Let the cognac bubble until reduced, and add the brown sugar Turn down the heat and cook until the onions caramelize.

In another sauté pan, melt the butter over medium heat, and sauté the mushrooms until soft. Season with salt.

ASSEMBLE THE BEEF BOURGIGNON: Stir the bacon, onions, and mushrooms into the stew. Stir in the chocolate until it melts. Remove the bouquet garnis and give the stew a last-minute taste, adjusting with salt and pepper as needed.

For serving, choose buttered noodles, crusty French bread, or herbed potatoes.

. . . .

✳ **HIP TIP:** *This recipe calls for braising the dish for 3 hours at 275°F, but the time and temperature aren't set in stone. It will cook beautifully at 300°F for 2–3 hours, or even at 225°F for an entire day, while you enjoy a walk in the park or a great book. The wonderful smells wafting from the oven will remind you that it's there.*

TARTE TATIN

The epitome of casual elegance, apples are cooked in caramel and baked under a flaky pastry. At serving time, it is flipped upside-down in glorious splendor.

Puff pastry	*1 sheet, thawed*
Apples	*4 (try slightly tart apples like Braeburn, or Bosc pears)*
Sugar	*1/2 cup*
Butter	*4 tablespoons*

Grab a 10-inch cast-iron skillet or oven-proof pan. Roll out the puff pastry on a floured surface and cut a circle a little larger than your pan. No need to be exact. Pop the pastry in the fridge to chill.

Core and cut the apples into sixths—leave the skin on for color, texture, and nutrition. Melt the sugar and butter in the skillet over high heat and allow to caramelize until light brown. Turn off the flame and arrange the apples in imperfect circles over the caramel. At this point, you can assemble the tarte and bake right away, or keep it on your stovetop to bake later, so that it can be served warm.

Preheat oven to 375°F.

Place the puff pastry over the apples, tucking in the sides. Poke small slits through the top with a paring knife to allow steam to escape during baking.

Pop the skillet in the oven and bake until the pastry is golden, 20–30 minutes. Let rest for 2–3 minutes.

Place a sturdy plate or round cutting board upside-down on the top of the tarte. Flip the skillet with conviction, holding the plate tightly against the pan. *Et voilà!*

Serve with crème fraîche glacée (recipe follows).

⁎ HIP TIP: *What makes this dessert even more magnificent is its portability! Once the apples in caramel have cooled, cover with the puff pastry and bring to your friend's house for a show-stopping dessert. Just chill the tart before baking so the puff pastry is cold when it hits the oven. Bake shortly before serving and flip to oohs and ahhhs.*

CRÈME FRAÎCHE GLACÉE

Instead of ice cream or whipped cream, we love to accompany this tarte with a tangy glacée. The flavors contrast beautifully and the preparation is a snap!

Crème fraîche	*2 cups (16 ounces)*
Buttermilk	*2 cups*
Lemon	*1, zested and juiced*
Vanilla bean paste	*1 tablespoon*
Sugar	*1¼ cups*

Blend all the ingredients in a blender or food processor until smooth. Chill.

About 20 minutes before serving (when the tarte goes into the oven), churn in an ice cream maker. This is nicest served fresh out of the ice cream maker before it has a chance to harden in the freezer.

HIP TIP: Once you taste the glacée, you'll be on the lookout for any excuse to make it again. It's wonderful with a fruit crumble, a fruit compote, or even something simple, like poached plums with cinnamon and vanilla.

MY BIG FAT GREEK DINNER PARTY

Can you say, "Mmmm ... **meze**"? Laden your table with small plates from Mediterranean islands filled with mid-afternoon snacking, sipping, and talking.

The pace is leisurely, the content simple. These full flavors won't weigh you down, but they'll nourish your body and spirit! Richness abounds from healthy olive oil, sunshine from plentiful lemons, and salt from the sea—all these ingredients are ever-present on a Greek table.

Much of this meal can be prepared in advance. It's a fair amount of work, so keep some ouzo on hand for sustenance. **Opa!**

GREECE

MENU

SAUTÉED HALLOUMI WITH OUZO

SPANIKOPITA

GRILLED VEGGIE SALAD

RACK OF LAMB WITH TZATZIKI

BAKLAVA

*serves 6

SAUTÉED HALLOUMI WITH OUZO

Squeaky halloumi cheese is magical. It can be grilled, fried, or sautéed without melting—even engulfed in flames, it will retain its shape! It pairs perfectly with ouzo.

Olive oil	2 tablespoons
Halloumi	1/2 pound, sliced
Parsley	1 small handful, chopped
Capers	1 teaspoon, roughly chopped
Lemon juice	from 1/2 lemon

TRADITIONAL METHOD: Heat a swirl of olive oil in a hot skillet over medium-high heat. Sauté the halloumi on both sides until golden. Cut into bite-sized pieces and transfer to a serving plate. Scatter with parsley, capers, a squeeze of lemon, and perhaps an extra drizzle of olive oil. Serve while hot.

PYRO METHOD: Follow steps above. Drizzle with a shot of ouzo. Ignite as you serve.

⁕ HIP TIP: *For a wonderful ouzo that even the ouzo-suspicious will enjoy, pour into ice-filled glasses and top with water. With a 1:1 ratio of water to ouzo, you can place bets you'll turn them into ouzo-lovers.*

SPANIKOPITA

Different from the norm, these mini spanikopita are light, airy, and fresh with lemon zest!

FILLING

Frozen spinach	8 ounces, thawed and squeezed of excess liquid
Garlic	2 cloves, chopped
Lemon zest	from 1 lemon
Nutmeg	1/4 teaspoon, freshly grated with a Microplane
Feta cheese	1/2 cup, crumbled
Parmesan cheese	1/2 cup, finely grated
Pine nuts	1/3 cup, toasted

PASTRY

Butter	4–5 tablespoons, melted
Phyllo	12 sheets, thawed

MAKE THE FILLING: Combine the spinach, garlic, zest, and nutmeg. Stir in the feta, parmesan, and pine nuts. Taste, and season with a little fresh ground pepper. Salt isn't necessary, since the cheeses are salty.

ASSEMBLE THE PASTRIES: Lay a single sheet of phyllo on a flat surface. Brush the sheet with melted butter. Fold in half, lengthwise, and then again. Brush a little more butter on the phyllo, and place a heaping spoonful of filling near the right corner. Fold the corner so that it makes a triangle. Continue folding until the edges are completely sealed (see the photos on page 67). Don't worry if the phyllo tears occasionally. Repeat with the remaining filling and phyllo. Brush the tops of the pastries with a little more butter. These can be refrigerated or frozen to bake later.

When you're ready to bake the pastries, preheat oven to 400°F. Bake for 15–20 minutes until golden brown and crispy. Allow to cool for a couple of minutes, and serve scattered with any fresh herbs you have on hand.

✳ HIP TIP: *Put extra spanikopita filling to good use by tossing into piping hot pasta. Add a little cream to loosen the mixture, stir into the pasta, and your dinner is done!*

GRILLED VEGGIE SALAD

Roasted onions add a lovely hint of sweetness that complements the bitter eggplant and zucchini. Basil, garlic, and Maldon salt make the flavors pop.

Eggplant	2, sliced into rounds (1/4 inch thick)
Zucchini	6, sliced lengthwise (1/4 inch thick)
Olive oil	3–4 tablespoons
Red onions	3, cut into eighths
Cognac	1/2 cup
Balsamic vinegar	1/2 teaspoon
Brown sugar	1 teaspoon
Thyme	1 sprig, leaves removed from stem (oregano is a good substitute)
Red peppers	3, roasted, peeled and seeded, and sliced (or use roasted red peppers in a jar)
Garlic	5–6 cloves, finely chopped
Basil	1 bunch, leaves removed from stems and sliced
Maldon salt	to finish

Brush the eggplant and zucchini with olive oil. Place on a hot grill until marks appear and the veggies are soft, about 5 minutes a side.

Preheat oven to 400°F. Heat a swirl or two of olive oil in an oven-safe pan over high. Caramelize the onions until nicely browned, 25–30 minutes. Splash in the cognac (look out for flames!), and cook until most of the liquid has evaporated. Stir in the vinegar, brown sugar, and thyme. Transfer the onions to the oven and cook until soft, about 20 minutes.

Toss the eggplant, zucchini, onions, and peppers in a large bowl with the garlic and basil. Add a swirl of olive oil so the flavors come together. Just before serving, add Maldon salt to taste.

✳ HIP TIP: Don't have a grill? Brush the eggplant and zucchini slices with olive oil, place on a cookie sheet, and bake in a 450°F oven until browned and cooked through.

RACK OF LAMB

The gorgeous presentation of this rack of lamb makes it the perfect centerpiece to your meze feast! Praise Dionysus and serve with a hearty red wine, like cabernet sauvignon.

Garlic	*8 cloves, chopped*
Rosemary	*3–4 stems, leaves removed from stem and chopped*
Lemon zest	*from 2 lemons*
Rack of lamb	*2 racks (each about 1½ pounds), trimmed of fat and gently scored*
Maldon salt	*to finish*

MAKE THE RUB: Combine the garlic, rosemary, and zest in a bowl. Rub it all over the lamb. Place in a container, seal with plastic wrap, and pop in the fridge for 3 hours, up to overnight.

COOK THE LAMB: Preheat oven to 425°F. Sear the lamb on all sides, either on the stovetop over high heat or on a hot grill. Transfer to the oven and roast until perfectly rare and juicy, 15–20 minutes. Insert your knife between the bones and slice into portions. If you find that the meat needs a little more cooking, throw the pieces in the oven for another few minutes. Allow to rest for a quick minute before sprinkling with Maldon salt. Serve with tzatziki (recipe following).

✴ **HIP TIP:** *If rack of lamb isn't available or is too expensive, a platter piled high with skewers of lamb, chicken, or veggies is just as impressive!*

TZATZIKI

Tzatziki—so fun to say, so easy to make, so delicious to *eat!*

English cucumber	*1, seeded and grated, squeezed of excess liquid*
Greek yogurt	*2 cups*
Dill	*1 handful, chopped*
Garlic	*2 cloves, finely minced*
Mint	*2–3 sprigs, chopped*
Coriander seed	*1 tablespoon, toasted and crushed*
Almond meal	*1/2 cup (for an added twist)*
Lemon juice	*from 1½–2 lemons*

Stir together all the ingredients. Taste, adjust the seasoning with salt and pepper, and enjoy with your lamb!

....

✳ HIP TIP: This recipe uses English cucumber, because it has an edible skin. Four reasons why we love the peel: 1. it has all the nutrients, 2. it offers great texture, 3. it gives a beautiful color, and 4. you don't have to peel anything!

BAKLAVA

After such an extravagant meal, a little taste of sweet baklava is all you need to transport you to the heights of Mt. Olympus.

PASTRY

Butter	8 tablespoons, melted
Phyllo	1/2 pack, thawed and trimmed to the size of your pan

FILLING

Walnuts	1 cup, chopped
Pistachios	1 cup, chopped

SYRUP

Sugar	1 cup
Lemon juice	from 1/2 lemon
Orange juice	from 1/2 orange
Cinnamon	2 sticks
Whole cloves	6
Whole nutmeg	a few scrapes with a Microplane
Cardamom pods	6, crushed
Honey	2/3 cup

ASSEMBLE THE BAKLAVA: Preheat oven to 350°F.

Brush some melted butter into the bottom of a shallow, medium-sized baking dish. Dip your pastry brush back into the butter, tap off excess, and brush onto a single sheet of phyllo. Place the brushed sheet onto the bottom of the dish and repeat until you have about 10 layers of phyllo. Sprinkle 1/2 of the nuts evenly over the dough. Repeat. Cover the final layer of nuts with at least 5 sheets of buttered phyllo. Cut the baklava into approximately 24 diamond shapes. Bake until golden, about 45 minutes.

MAKE THE SYRUP: Combine the sugar with 2/3 cup water, lemon and orange juices, cinnamon, cloves, nutmeg, and cardamom in a saucepan over medium-high heat. Simmer the mixture for 5–10 minutes—it should smell heavenly. Remove from the heat and swirl in the honey until dissolved. Strain into a vessel with a pouring spout.

When the baklava is out of the oven, pour the syrup all over the top. It will run into all the cut edges and sides of the pan. You may not need all of it, as the baklava should not be submerged. Allow to stand for at least 3 hours (but best overnight) so the nuts can absorb the syrup.

Baklava improves with age. It keeps really well for several days, though refrigeration can dry it out, so simply cover and leave at room temperature.

⋆ **HIP TIP:** *Have fun with your syrup, adjusting it to suit your mood. Cayenne is a beautiful fiery addition, as are slivers of fresh ginger. Rose water gives a floral pop. Extra syrup is delicious stirred into herbal tea.*

1001 ARABIAN NIGHTS

Channel your inner Scheherazade and weave a dramatic tale with food that your guests will never forget. Lavish upon them your attention and grace, bestowing the plenitude of these sumptuous dishes. With effortless charm, lay fragrant plates filled with exotic flavors. Delight them with a dish laden with jewels—golden threads, shining rubies, and deep emeralds—that promises wealth and happiness to those who partake of it.

IRAN

MENU

HERB-STUDDED MEATBALLS WITH CUCUMBER YOGURT SAUCE

CHICKEN STEWED WITH POMEGRANATE AND WALNUTS
OR
CHICKEN WITH JEWELED RICE

ROSE WATER AND CARDAMOM CRÈME BRÛLÉE

✳ serves 6

HERB-STUDDED MEATBALLS

These little meatballs are bursting with fresh flavor from the chopped herbs.

Ground beef	1 ½ pounds (or use lamb, or a 50/50 mix)
Garlic	3 cloves, minced
Mint	1 handful, chopped
Parsley	1 handful, chopped
Scallions	4, chopped
Olive oil	2 teaspoons
Lemon	1/2

Mix together the beef, garlic, mint, parsley, and scallions. Season with a teaspoon or two of salt and a few grinds of pepper. Shape into balls, about the size of golf balls.

Pour a swirl of olive oil into a large sauté pan over high heat. Add the meatballs and cook till nicely browned on all sides and cooked through, 8–10 minutes. Transfer to a serving dish and deglaze the hot pan with a hearty squeeze of lemon. Pour over the meatballs and serve alongside maast-o khiar (recipe following), toasted lavash, and a fresh green salad.

✳ HIP TIP: Next time you're planning to grill plain hamburgers, make them Persian-style by throwing in some garlic and a few handfuls of herbs!

MAAST-O KHIAR: CUCUMBER YOGURT SAUCE

Traditionally, chopped tomato is added to this dish. Instead, we love to add a handful of walnut meal, which creates texture and depth.

Persian cucumbers	8, seeded, grated, and squeezed of excess liquid
Greek yogurt	1 cup
Lemon juice	from 1 lemon
Walnuts	1/3 cup, ground to a fine meal (store-bought almond meal is a great substitute)
Maldon salt	to finish

FOR SERVING:
Toasted lavash (flatbread)
Green salad

Stir together all of the ingredients. Finish with a sprinkle of Maldon salt and a twist of black pepper.

··

✳ HIP TIP: *Lavash bread has become so popular, you can find it at most grocery stores. Use it for rolled sandwiches, or adorn with toppings and bake to enjoy a lavash pizza!*

KHORESHT FESENJAAN: CHICKEN STEWED WITH POMEGRANATE AND WALNUTS

This stew is so unique your guests will remember it for years to come. As it cooks, the walnuts literally melt into the stew, giving it a rich flavor. Paired with sour pomegranate, this dish brings the joy of the unexpected.

STEW

Walnuts	1 ½ cups, ground to a fine meal
Pomegranate molasses	3/4 cup, plus more for sour palates
Onions	2, finely chopped
Butter	2 tablespoons, plus 1 teaspoon
Chicken thighs	12, skinless and boneless, cut into chunks (about 3 pounds)
Chicken stock	3–4 cups
Sugar	1/4 cup
Mint	1 small handful, chopped
Parsley	1 small handful, chopped
Scallions	3–4, chopped
Greek yogurt	1/3 cup (sour cream, crème fraîche, or cream is also great)

FOR SERVING

Basmati rice	3 cups, cooked and still warm

Gently toast the walnuts in a heavy-bottomed pan over medium heat, stirring continuously. Once they turn a light shade of brown and release their perfume (about 5 minutes), stir in the pomegranate molasses and 1 cup of hot water. Lower the heat to medium-low and cook, stirring occasionally, until the walnuts begin to dissolve and become creamy, 15–20 minutes. The mixture should have the consistency of a thick sauce. If it becomes too pasty, add more hot water.

While the walnuts are cooking down, sauté the onions in 2 tablespoons of butter over medium heat, until translucent. Add the chicken and sauté until the chicken turns white.

Add the chicken and onions to the walnut mixture. Pour in enough stock so that everything is immersed. Bring to a boil and immediately reduce the heat to low. Simmer for 20 minutes, so that the walnuts can begin breaking down and melting into the stew.

Next, taste the stew! It will most likely taste mildly sour. You'll want to add the sugar, so that you can add even more fabulous pomegranate flavor without making your mouth pucker. If the extra pomegranate makes it too sour, add a little more sugar. It's a fun balancing game to get the flavors just right! Salt to taste.

Continue to cook on low heat until the walnuts completely break down, another 15–20 minutes. This dish benefits from extra time on the stovetop.

Melt the remaining teaspoon of butter in a pan over high heat. Sauté the mint, parsley, and scallions until bright and fragrant. Stir into the stew. Finish by stirring in a swirl of yogurt, taste once more, and serve with warm basmati rice.

....

✳ HIP TIP: *Pomegranate molasses is a fantastic ingredient to have on hand. It brings zing to salad dressings, pucker to mojitos, and magic to bulghur wheat with fennel, parsley, and pecans.*

SHIRIN-POLOW: CHICKEN WITH JEWELED RICE

Traditionally served at weddings and other very special occasions, this jewel-studded rice brings good fortune to those who eat it. Even more special is the famous *tah dig*, a crisp layer of crust on the bottom of the dish.

Basmati rice	3 cups (jasmine rice is a great substitute)
Onions	2 large, chopped
Butter	2 tablespoons, plus 4 tablespoons
Chicken thighs	12, skinless and boneless, cut into large chunks (about 3 pounds)
Saffron threads	1 teaspoon (your golden threads!)
Sugar	1/4 cup
Salt	1/4 cup
Flaked almonds	1/2 cup (your diamonds!)
Pistachios	1/2 cup (your emeralds!)
Orange peel	from 2 oranges, ribboned with a cocktail zester (your topazes!)
Barberries	1/2 cup (dried cranberries are a good substitute) (your rubies!)

COOK THE RICE: Wash the rice thoroughly, then soak in water for 1 hour. Drain, then pour into the heaviest-bottomed pot you have, covering with 5 cups of water. Crank up the heat, bring to a boil, immediately turn off the heat, and cover. Let it rest for at least 15 minutes, or until all your preparations below are done and you're ready for the rice. (Ideally, it should be just underdone, since it continues to cook after you assemble the dish.)

COOK THE CHICKEN: Sauté the onions in 2 tablespoons of butter over medium heat until translucent. Add the chicken and sauté until it turns white. Add 3 cups of water and bring to a boil. Turn off the heat, and remove the chicken and onions from the water with a slotted spoon. Don't worry about getting every last onion.

FLAVOR THE BROTH: While the chicken broth is still warm, stir in the saffron—it will turn the liquid a vibrant yellow and smell heavenly. Stir in the sugar and salt. Taste! It will be quite sweet and salty indeed—you need this to flavor the rice.

JEWEL THE RICE: Reserve 1 cup of rice and stir the flaked almonds, pistachios, orange peels, and barberries into the remaining rice.

ASSEMBLE THE DISH: Melt 4 more tablespoons of butter in a non-stick sauté pan over medium heat till it sizzles. Scatter the reserved plain rice over the butter. Layer in half the jeweled rice, top with all of the chicken and onions, and cover with the other half of the jeweled rice. Press down on the rice to sandwich it all nicely. Pour the saffron broth all over the top. In about 10 minutes, the steam coming off the pan will stop. Turn the heat to low and allow the *tah dig to* form. In several minutes, you'll smell the bittersweet aroma of browning rice and hear it crackle!

Check the *tah dig* by pushing a spatula down the side of the rice and lifting a bit. If it looks crusty and brown, it's ready to be turned out. Place a sturdy non-breakable plate, or a round cutting board, atop the pan. With one hand supporting the plate and another holding the pan, take a deep breath and flip with conviction! Gently lift the pan off the rice, using a spatula to loosen any *tah dig* pieces that stick. Serve to your thrilled guests.

✳ HIP TIP: *Persians are masters of cooking rice. First, they rinse it to remove excess starch, yielding perfectly fluffy rice. It is then soaked before cooking, so it will soften and cook evenly. Then the cooked rice is rinsed and steamed again to remove any additional excess starch. We find the first two steps are sufficient to ensure impeccable rice each time.*

ROSE WATER AND CARDAMOM CRÈME BRÛLÉE

This elegant dessert is the perfect finish to the meal. And you get to light things on fire!

Egg yolks	5
Sugar	1/2 cup, plus 6 teaspoons
Heavy cream	2 cups
Cardamom	seeds from a few pods, removed and crushed
Cinnamon	1 stick
Vanilla bean paste	1 teaspoon
Rose water	2 teaspoons
Rose petals	for garnish (use pesticide-free roses from your garden)

Preheat oven to 325°F.

Whisk the egg yolks and sugar until just combined. Place the cream in a pot over medium heat, and stir in the cardamom and cinnamon. When bubbles form along the edge, turn the heat to low and stir, inhaling the spicy aroma. When the spices are infused, strain the hot cream into the eggs. Whisk to combine. Stir in the vanilla bean paste and rose water. Sample it! Because who knows: maybe you're the type who likes a more floral flavor.

Fill 6 ramekins (6- or 7-ounce are perfect) equally with the custard. Place in an oven-proof pan, pouring in enough hot water to come about halfway up the sides of the ramekins. (At Hipcooks, we pour the water after we put the pan in the oven, to avoid spills.) Bake for about 30 minutes until the custards are just set (the tops will still jiggle slightly). Cool in the fridge for at least 2 hours, and up to several days. (If you're making well in advance, cover with plastic wrap.)

How do you like your caramel? For a thick layer that cracks when tapped with a spoon, sprinkle the top of a custard with a heaping teaspoon of sugar. Gently shake, so the sugar makes an even layer. For a perfect lacy top, turn the ramekin upside down and tap out any excess sugar onto its neighbor. Repeat with all the ramekins. Now comes the fun part! Torch the brûlée until golden (we use an inexpensive plumber's torch from a hardware store). Wait for the tops to cool and harden, top with rose petals, and serve.

· ·

✳ HIP TIP: *Varying the flavor of crème brûlée couldn't be simpler. Instead of the spices, infuse the cream with jasmine or chai tea, or add some Grand Marnier, grated ginger, and orange. Try a few squares of dark chocolate and a shot of espresso. Your imagination is the limit!*

SHORTCUT TO NIRVANA

In India there's an expression that when food is delicious it's because the person preparing it has sweet hands. Joyfully use your hands when adding your spices: a dash of this one, a sprinkle of that one. Tap into your inner guru for the perfect amounts. Taste and adjust until you are elevated to a higher level of consciousness!

Hop on the nonstop, all-India karma train. This food is to die for. Then you reincarnate, and die for it again!

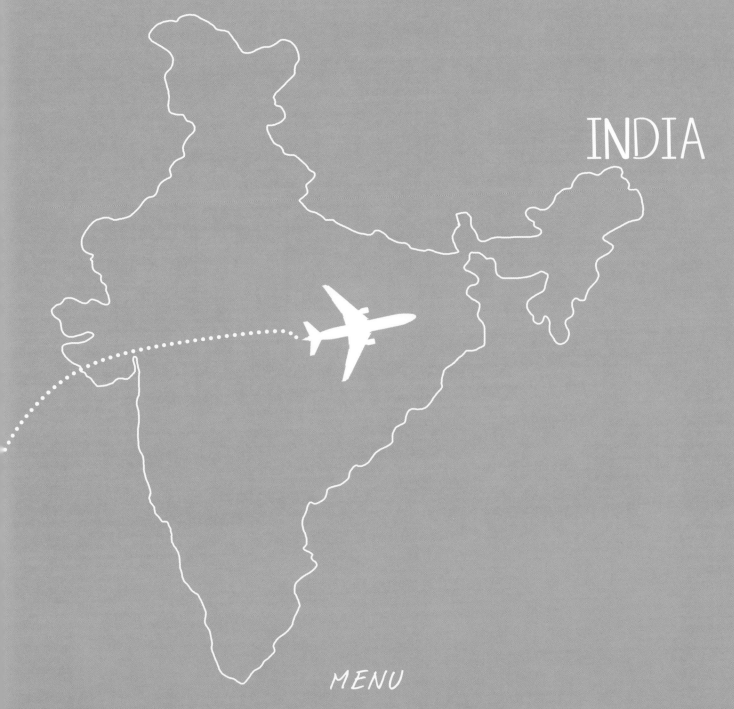

INDIA

MENU
PAPADUMS WITH THREE FLAVORFUL SAUCES
SAAG PANEER
CHICKEN TIKKA MASALA WITH FANCY BASMATI RICE
MANGO, GINGER, AND LIME SORBET

* serves 6

PAPADUMS

Papadums are light-as-air flatbreads made out of chickpea flour. Buy them dried and cook just before serving.

Oil	*2–3 cups, depending on the size of your skillet*
Papadums	*1 package (you'll need about 36 papadums)*

Heat an inch of oil in a wok or medium skillet—you want the oil hot, but not smoking. Using tongs, dip a papadum into the oil. Fry until puffy and golden, 20–30 seconds. Remove from the oil, and drain on paper towels. Repeat with the remaining papadums.

⚹ HIP TIP: *Healthier than frying, you can poof the papadums directly over an open flame. Try it!*

THREE FLAVORFUL SAUCES

This little trifecta of sauces bursts with flavor sensations! The mango chutney is sweet and sour, the green sauce is spicy and—ah—the the raita is cooling!

MANGO CHUTNEY

Mangos	2, peeled, pitted, and chopped (use frozen when not in season)
Brown sugar	1/4 cup
Apple cider vinegar	1/2 cup
Raisins	1/4 cup (dried currants or cranberries are also lovely)
Garlic	1 clove, thinly sliced
Ginger	1/2 thumb-sized piece, peeled and grated with a Microplane
Star anise	1
Cinnamon	1 stick
Whole cloves	3

Bring the mangos, brown sugar, and vinegar to a simmer in a heavy saucepan over medium heat. Lower heat, and stir in the remaining ingredients. Cook, stirring occasionally, until the mangos are very soft and the chutney is light brown and jammy, about 45 minutes. You may need to add a bit of water during this process if your pan becomes too dry—no more than half a cup. Fish out the star anise, cinnamon, and cloves. Taste and adjust for sweetness, adding more vinegar if it tastes too sweet, more sugar if it makes your mouth pucker.

SPICY GREEN SAUCE

Mint leaves	2 bunches, stems removed
Cilantro	1 bunch, stems removed
Scallions	6, chopped
Jalapeño peppers	2, halved and seeded
Lime juice	from 1 lime
Frozen shredded coconut	1/2 cup (or use dried unsweetened coconut)

In a blender or food processor, blend all of the ingredients with 3 tablespoons of water until smooth. Scrape the sides and bottom with a spatula once or twice to make sure everything blends evenly. Taste and add salt as needed. If it's too spicy, add more coconut or lime. If it isn't spicy enough, you know what to do!

RAITA: CUCUMBER YOGURT SAUCE

English cucumber	1, seeded and grated, squeezed of excess liquid
Tomatoes	2, seeded and chopped
Greek yogurt	2 cups
Lemon juice	from 1/2 lemon
Cumin seeds	1 teaspoon, freshly toasted and ground
Garam masala	1 small pinch, if you like

Combine the cucumber, tomatoes, yogurt, lemon juice, and cumin. (No cumin in the house? Coriander is also delicious!) Taste and season with salt. As a finishing touch, add a sprinkle of garam masala on top.

....

✳ HIP TIP: *Leftover sauces are wonderful to sneak into a sandwich. Turkey breast with mango chutney, cucumber with spicy green sauce, roast beef with raita—now **that's** a sammich!*

SAAG PANEER

Using frozen spinach means that you can enjoy this dish in a matter of minutes!

Butter	3 tablespoons
Onion	1, chopped
Ginger	2 thumb-sized pieces, peeled and chopped
Garlic	7 cloves, chopped
Cumin seeds	1 tablespoon, freshly toasted and ground
Paneer	1 pound, cubed
Frozen chopped spinach	2 (16-ounce) bags, thawed
Crushed red pepper flakes	to taste (or chile powder instead)
Garam masala	1 teaspoon
Cream	4–6 tablespoons, if desired

Melt butter in a sauté pan over medium-high heat. Sauté the onions, ginger, and garlic until the onion turns translucent.

Add the cumin—the pan will be wonderfully fragrant. Stir in the paneer and cook for several minutes. Add the spinach and cook until it is warmed through. Now comes the fun: tasting the dish! It'll need salt and pepper for sure. If you love a little heat, add a sprinkle of pepper flakes. Otherwise, the warming (but not spicy) addition of garam masala is beautiful.

Finish by stirring in a swirl of cream, to be naughty *and* nice.

....

✳ HIP TIP: *We often make a quick version of this recipe as a late-night dinner after teaching class. Simply sauté the spinach in a bit of olive oil with loads of garlic and ginger and you're eating a super-food, super-fast!*

CHICKEN TIKKA MASALA WITH FANCY BASMATI RICE

Butter plus sour cream in this recipe makes for a very warm and rich stew. In class, we call it dessert!

MARINADE

Yogurt	2 cups
Garlic	12 cloves, chopped and divided in half
Ginger	2 thumb-sized pieces, peeled, chopped, and divided in half
Coriander seeds	2 teaspoons, toasted and ground
Paprika	1 teaspoon, plus 1 tablespoon
Turmeric	1 teaspoon
Chicken thighs	2 pounds, boneless and skinless, cut into bite-sized pieces

CURRY

Butter	6 tablespoons
Onions	2, finely chopped
Ripe tomatoes	2 pounds, finely chopped
Tomato paste	2 tablespoons
Sour cream	2–4 tablespoons (heavy cream is a good substitute)
Cumin seeds	1 teaspoon, freshly toasted and ground
Cilantro	1 bunch, chopped

RICE

Onion	1, chopped
Olive oil	1–2 tablespoons
Star anise	2
Cardamom	2–3 pods
Cumin seeds	1–2 teaspoons
Basmati rice	2 cups

MAKE THE MARINADE: Combine the yogurt, half the chopped garlic and ginger, coriander, a teaspoon of paprika, and the turmeric. Coat the chicken and place in a covered container. Pop in the fridge for at least an hour, up to a day.

Preheat oven to 450°.

Place the chicken on a baking tray and pop in the oven until cooked through, about 15 minutes.

MAKE THE CURRY: Melt the butter in a heavy pot over medium-high heat. Add the onions and the remaining garlic and ginger, stirring to coat. Sauté until the onions are translucent. Stir in a tablespoon of paprika along with the tomatoes and tomato paste. Add the chicken and simmer for at least 40 minutes. Taste the sauce; salt generously. Finish with a swirl of sour cream, a healthy pinch of cumin seeds, and loads of chopped cilantro.

MAKE THE RICE: Why serve your dish with plain rice when it takes no time to turn it into something fancy? In a heavy-bottomed pot over medium-high heat, sauté the onion in a swirl or two of oil. Stir in the star anise, cardamom pods, and cumin. When the onion is translucent, add the rice, and toast for a few seconds. Add 3 cups of water and bring to a boil. Turn heat to low, cover, and simmer for 5 minutes. Move the rice to the back part of your stove to steam while you cook the rest of the meal. It will finish cooking and stay delightfully warm in the pot. Remove cardamom pods and star anise before serving.

⋇ HIP TIP: Why chicken thigh? Because they're juicy, goosey! Chicken breast is a healthy alternative, but we prefer this dish to be luscious.

MANGO, GINGER, AND LIME SORBET

With a high-speed blender like a Vitamix, you can make fresh sorbet in a flash—all you need is frozen fruit! The traditional method, of course, also works for this refreshing finish to your spicy meal.

Frozen mango	*8 ounces, thawed or left frozen depending on method*
Water	*1 cup*
Ginger	*1/2 thumb-sized piece, grated with a Microplane*
Lime	*1, zested and juiced*
Coconut	*unsweetened dessicated, toasted, for garnish*

ICE CREAM MAKER METHOD: Blend all the ingredients in a blender or food processor until smooth. Chill. About 20 minutes before serving, churn in an ice-cream maker. This is nicest served fresh out of the ice cream maker, before it has a chance to harden in the freezer.

VITAMIX METHOD: To make this sorbet using your Vitamix, simply keep your mango frozen, and up the water to 2 cups. Add all the ingredients to the Vitamix and blend, using the plunger, until the sorbet is the perfect consistency. Serve immediately.

....

✳ HIP TIP: *Now that you've got it down pat—invent! Strawberry, black pepper, and basil sorbet is summery and fresh. Or blueberry, cardamom, and vanilla, with a swirl of cream at the end. We love peach and mint with a touch of balsamic. Any type of fruit works well, and you can tinker by adding fresh herbs, spices, or condiments. The road to Nirvana is paved with fun!*

THAI ONE ON

Why, oh why, is Thai food so very delicious? Thai chefs have a sneaky secret that all cooks can learn from—they compose each dish with a very purposeful combination of sweet, sour, bitter, spicy, and salty. And oh, how they revel in the task!

The spring rolls in this chapter are the perfect springboard for experimenting with combining flavors, Thai-style. Carrots are sweet, lime is sour, bell peppers are bitter, ginger and garlic are spicy, and fish sauce is salty! Add the ingredients one at a time, tasting after each. Observe how the lime dampens the bitterness; notice how the fish sauce pulls everything together; feel the spice hit your taste buds last, tingling on the tongue.

Let anything you cook be improved by thinking like a Thai gourmand. Is your pesto too salty (whoops!)? Balance the flavor with sweetness from nuts. Is your marinara sauce lackluster? Jazz it up with a touch of Tabasco for spice, or a hint of salt from, dare we say, fish sauce! Umami guaranteed.

THAILAND

MENU

VEGGIE SPRING ROLLS

GREEN CURRY WITH EGGPLANT AND MUSHROOMS
OR
RED CURRY WITH CHICKEN AND CASHEWS

COCONUT STICKY RICE

FORBIDDEN RICE WITH COCONUT MILK

*serves 6

VEGGIE SPRING ROLLS

These colorful rolls are easy to prepare. Get all your ingredients ready beforehand and assemble just before serving so they burst with sassy flavor.

FILLING

Red pepper	1/2, thinly sliced
Carrots	1 cup, grated (about 3 carrots)
Beets	1/2 cup, peeled and grated (this is about 1 small beet's worth)
Bean sprouts	1/2 cup
Scallions	6, thinly sliced, green parts only
Lime juice	from 3 limes
Fish sauce	2 tablespoons
Mint	1 handful, chopped
Ginger	1/2 thumb-sized piece, peeled
Garlic	1 clove
Olive oil	1 teaspoon

ROLLS

Thai spring roll wrappers	12 (8.5 inch) circles
Shiso	1 bunch, stems removed (basil is a great substitute)

MAKE THE FILLING: Combine the peppers, carrots, beets, sprouts, scallions, lime juice, fish sauce, and mint. Using a Microplane, grate in the ginger and garlic. Stir in a bit of olive oil, and inhale the freshness. Taste! If it needs more salt from the fish sauce, spice from the garlic and ginger, or sour from the lime, adjust with glee.

ASSEMBLE THE ROLLS: Bring a skillet filled with water to a boil over high heat. Turn off the heat, then dip one wrapper in the water until just barely soft, and lay it on a clean surface. Place a large spoonful of veggies in the middle, tuck in the edges like a burrito, and roll! At the last roll, tuck in a shiso leaf, pretty side down, for color and flavor. Repeat with the remaining filling and wrappers.

....

✳ **HIP TIP:** *Variations on spring rolls are endless! Add cooked shrimp or grilled chicken or, for that matter, just about any leftover from your fridge—sliced flank steak, barbecued pork, or extra veggies. Or make it simple—a roll with nothing but Thai glass noodles, basil, and fish sauce is tasty as can be.*

GREEN CURRY WITH EGGPLANT AND MUSHROOMS

This is the fresher and sassier of the two curries. Instead of eggplant and mushrooms you can pair this curry paste with shrimp, bell peppers and snap peas—or whatever you like!

CURRY PASTE

Coriander seeds	1 teaspoon, toasted
Cumin seeds	1/2 teaspoon, toasted
Black peppercorns	1/4 teaspoon, toasted
Galangal	1/2 thumb-sized piece, peeled and chopped
Lemongrass	2 tablespoons, chopped (lower third only)
Lime leaves	3, stems removed
Cilantro	1/2 bunch, leaves removed from stems, reserving both
Shallots	2 small (or use 1/2 red onion)
Garlic	2 cloves
Shrimp paste	1 teaspoon (or use fish sauce)
Fresh turmeric	1 thumb-sized piece, peeled (or 1 teaspoon dried)
Thai green chilies	10–20 (depending on how hot you like it!), stems removed
Thai basil	1 large bunch, stems removed
Lime juice	from 1/2 lime
Fish sauce	3–6 tablespoons
Grapeseed oil	2–4 tablespoons
Japanese eggplant	2, halved and sliced into half-moons
Shiitake mushrooms	2 cups, stemmed and sliced (reconstituted dried shiitakes are also great)
Coconut milk	1 (15-ounce) can

MAKE THE CURRY PASTE: Grind the coriander, cumin, and peppercorns in a food processor. Add the galangal, lemongrass, 2 lime leaves, cilantro stems, shallots, garlic, shrimp paste, turmeric, chilies, and most of the Thai basil, reserving some for garnish. Puree until smooth. Add the lime juice and 3 tablespoons of fish sauce to start. You may need to add a tablespoon or two of grapeseed oil to encourage a smooth paste. Taste and adjust the flavorings as needed—more salt from the fish sauce, more sour from the lime, more spice from the chilies!

ASSEMBLE THE DISH: Sauté the eggplant and mushrooms in a swirl or two of grapeseed oil over medium-high heat. When beginning to brown, add the coconut milk, bring to a boil, then lower heat. Stir in the green curry paste, a little at a time, until you've reached your desired color and taste. Simmer until the veggies are soft. Taste for seasoning and adjust with additional fish sauce or lime juice as needed. Just before serving, garnish with the reserved cilantro and Thai basil, and a finely sliced lime leaf.

Serve with coconut sticky rice (recipe follows).

....

✻ **HIP TIP:** *Both of the curry pastes are incredibly versatile. Make plenty of extra for future meals. Green curry mixed into leftover basmati rice makes a quick meal on the go. Red curry is delightful to rub over a whole chicken before roasting.*

COCONUT STICKY RICE

This sweet, salty, and zesty rice is a crowd pleaser.

Thai sweet rice	*3 cups*
Coconut milk	*1 cup*
Lime zest	*from 1 lime*

SOAK THE RICE: Cover the rice with water and soak for at least 3 hours, up to overnight. Drain into a colander or sieve.

STEAM THE RICE: If you don't have a rice cooker with a steamer basket, a pot with a colander inside works just as well. Place the pot over low heat. Add just enough boiling water to almost touch the colander. Pour the rice in the colander, place over the water, cover, and steam away. The rice should take anywhere from 20–30 minutes, until tender.

When cooked, place the rice in a large bowl. Stir in the coconut milk, lime zest, and a pinch or two of salt. Marvel at how quickly the rice absorbs all the liquid—it just needs a minute or two. Spread the rice on a cookie sheet, pressing down to compact it. It will set as it cools.

Thirty minutes before serving, warm it in the oven on very low heat (200°F). When you're ready to serve, cut the rice into wedges.

HIP TIP: *The fun part of this recipe comes when you're adding coconut milk, lime zest, and salt until the proportions taste just right to you. Try not to eat all of it while tasting to perfection!*

RED CURRY WITH CHICKEN AND CASHEWS

This curry is worth the work—a warm and satisfying dish, perfectly comforting.

MARINADE

Fish sauce	2 tablespoons
Brown sugar	2 tablespoons, plus an extra pinch or two
Garlic	2 cloves, chopped
Ginger	1 thumb-sized piece, peeled and chopped
Curry powder	1 teaspoon
Chicken thighs	6–8, boneless and skinless

CURRY PASTE

Coriander seeds	1 tablespoon, toasted
Cardamom	4 pods, black seeds removed from husk and toasted
Black peppercorns	1/4 teaspoon, toasted
Galangal	1/2 thumb-sized piece, peeled and chopped
Lemongrass	2 tablespoons (lower third only), chopped
Lime leaves	2 leaves, stems removed
Cilantro	1/2 bunch, leaves removed from stems, reserving both
Shallots	2 small (or use 1/2 red onion)
Garlic	2 cloves
Shrimp paste	1 teaspoon (or use fish sauce)
Fresh turmeric	1 thumb-sized piece, peeled (or 1 teaspoon dried)
Thai red chilies	10–20 (depending on how hot you like it!), stems removed
Dried chiles	3 ancho, pasilla, or mulato, toasted, soaked in boiling water for at least 1 hour, and drained
Lime juice	from 1/2 lime
Cashews	2 cups, toasted
Grapeseed oil	1–2 tablespoons

MAKE THE MARINADE: Combine the fish sauce, brown sugar, garlic, ginger, and curry powder. Pour over the chicken, tossing to coat. Pop in the fridge for at least 3 hours, up to overnight.

MAKE THE CURRY: Grind the coriander, cardamom, and peppercorns in a food processor. Add the galangal, lemongrass, lime leaves, cilantro stems, shallots, garlic, shrimp paste, turmeric, and Thai chilies. Puree until smooth. De-stem and de-seed the dried chiles and add to the mix along with the lime juice. Process until very smooth. Add half of the cashews and pulse. You may need a tablespoon or two of grapeseed oil to encourage a smooth paste. Taste, and adjust flavorings as needed—more salt from some fish sauce, more sour from the lime, more spicy from the chilies! Perhaps a pinch of brown sugar? Whatever it needs to make you giddy with delight.

ASSEMBLE THE DISH: Sauté the chicken in a swirl of grapeseed oil over medium-high heat, until the chicken just starts to turn white. Stir in the red curry paste until it reaches your desired consistency. Add half a cup of water if you like a more liquid curry. Simmer for a good 15 minutes.

Taste and adjust with curry paste, lime juice, and salt or fish sauce, according to your love of fish sauce—ours is huge. Garnish with reserved cilantro leaves and remaining cashews.

Serve with coconut sticky rice (recipe on page 127).

* **HIP TIP:** *Can't resist the urge to take it over the top? Give in to temptation and add a splash of coconut milk!*

FORBIDDEN RICE WITH COCONUT MILK

The beautiful deep purple color of this exotic rice is so mesmerizing, you'll forget that it's so healthy. Because this rice has so much of its husk, it will cook to perfect "crunchiness."

Forbidden rice	2 cups (also called Thai black rice or sweet black rice)
Coconut milk	1 (15-ounce) can, or be sinful and use coconut cream instead
Brown sugar	1/3 cup
Vanilla bean paste	2 tablespoons
Almond flakes	1/2 cup, toasted

PREPARE THE RICE: Soak the rice in water for at least 3 hours, up to overnight. Drain.

STEAM THE RICE: If you don't have a rice maker with a steamer basket, a pot with a colander inside works just as well. Place the pot over low heat. Add just enough boiling water to almost touch the colander. Pour the rice in the colander, place over the water, cover, and steam away. The rice should take anywhere from 30–40 minutes, until tender.

ASSEMBLE THE DISH: Combine the rice with enough coconut milk to make it creamy. The rice will absorb most of the liquid. Stir in the brown sugar and vanilla bean paste, along with a pinch of salt.

Serve in individual bowls, topped with any extra coconut milk and a sprinkle of almond flakes.

HIP TIP: *Forbidden rice makes a perfect breakfast! Add fresh mango, strawberries, and blueberries in the summer; or dried cranberries and raisins in the winter.*

TURNING JAPANESE

Break out the chopsticks and roll that sushi! What could be better than getting everyone involved in the meal preparation? This party can take place in the kitchen, so your guests make, taste, and share one another's creations. A few strategically placed nibbles (like sashimi and inari skins) will tide over the hungriest (or least industrious) of guests.

Preparation is the key to pulling off a lively sushi party. Lay out all the ingredients in pretty bowls—think how an artist uses a palette—and give each guest a "station," with a sushi mat and water for dipping close by. Give a demonstration on how to roll sushi, then sit back and enjoy your friends' talents and the fruits of their labor!

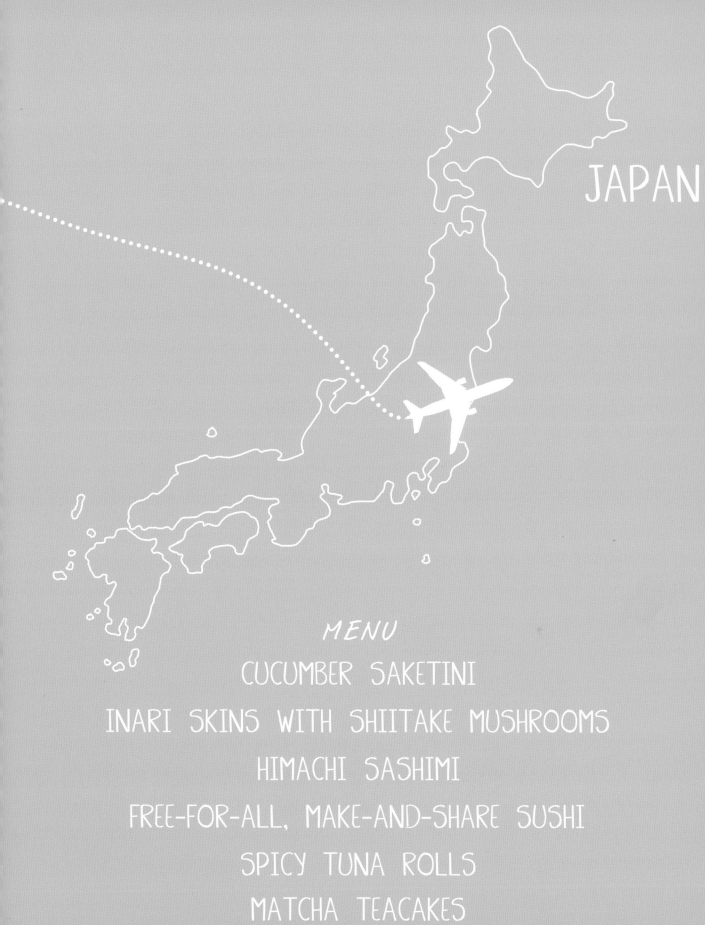

JAPAN

MENU
CUCUMBER SAKETINI
INARI SKINS WITH SHIITAKE MUSHROOMS
HIMACHI SASHIMI
FREE-FOR-ALL, MAKE-AND-SHARE SUSHI
SPICY TUNA ROLLS
MATCHA TEACAKES

✳ serves 12

CUCUMBER SAKETINI

For drinks, you can assemble a sake-tasting station with both filtered and unfiltered sakes to sample. A signature cocktail like this one can make your event special.

Sake	*2½ ounces*
Vodka	*1 ounce (gin is a fine substitute)*
Lemon juice	*from 1 lemon*
Japanese cucumber	*1 (1-inch) piece, grated with a Microplane, plus 1 thin slice for garnish*

In your hands or with a cheesecloth, squeeze the juice out of the grated cucumber. Since the cucumber is left unpeeled, the juice will be a very vibrant green, perfect for a gorgeous cocktail.

Fill a cocktail shaker halfway with ice and add the sake, vodka, lemon juice, and cucumber juice. Shake vigorously. Strain into a martini glass and garnish with a cucumber slice.

HIP TIP: *Instead of cucumber juice, try this cocktail with a jasmine pearl tea simple syrup (see the info on making flavored simple syrups on page 46) and garnish with a jasmine pearl.*

INARI SKINS WITH SHIITAKE MUSHROOMS

You can buy inari skins in the refrigerated section of Asian grocery stores. They are sweet little pockets made of fried bean curd and they work just as well for dessert as they do as appetizers.

Shiitake mushrooms	*12, thinly sliced*
Grapeseed oil	*1–2 tablespoons*
Soy sauce	*2–3 tablespoons*
Mirin	*2–3 tablespoons*
Balsamic vinegar	*1 tablespoon*
Scallions	*4–5 chopped, reserving some for garnish*
Inari skins	*24*
Cooked sushi rice	*1½ cups (see recipe on page 139)*

Sauté the shiitakes in a swirl or two of oil over medium-high heat. After the mushrooms have absorbed the oil, about 1 minute into cooking, add the soy sauce, mirin, and vinegar. Let the liquid reduce as the mushrooms finish cooking. Remove from the heat and toss in the scallions.

Open the inari skins and fill with a spoonful of sushi rice and a few mushrooms. Serve on a plate scattered with scallions.

✳ HIP TIP: *For a "not-too-sweet" treat, fill the inari skins halfway with sushi rice and top with fresh mango slices. Scatter with thinly sliced basil, and you'll have the perfect pop-in-your-mouth dessert.*

HIMACHI (YELLOWTAIL) SASHIMI

Melt-in-your-mouth fish needs very little adornment, and this simple recipe is a celebration of the *himachi* itself. Other types of fish work just as well with this delicate dressing. Try super-fresh raw scallops, halibut, or even snapper.

Premium fresh himachi	*1/2 pound, sliced thinly on a bias*
Ponzu	*2 tablespoons*
Scallions	*2 tablespoons, thinly sliced*

Arrange the sashimi in a pretty fashion across a plate. Sprinkle with ponzu and garnish with scallions.

HIP TIP: *Are you nervous about sashimi-ing the fish? The guy at the fish counter will be tickled to do it for you!*

SUSHI RICE

For the perfect sushi rice, make it no more than a few hours in advance. Be sure to use Japanese sushi rice, as other types of rice will not have the necessary starch to be "sticky."

Sushi rice	*4 cups, rinsed until water runs clear*
Water	*5¼ cups*
Seasoned rice vinegar	*3/4 cup*

MAKE THE RICE: Place the rice and water in a saucepan and soak for 30 minutes, then bring to a boil. Turn heat to low, cover, and cook for 10 minutes. Turn off the heat and let it rest, covered, for at least 15 minutes to finish cooking. Alternatively, you can cook the rice in a rice cooker after it has soaked.

SEASON THE RICE: Transfer the rice to a non-reactive bowl, fanning it to help remove excess moisture. A paddle-type spatula works best here. While the rice is still warm, but cool enough to touch, slowly pour the vinegar over the top, stirring gently until combined. Be careful not to over-mix. Cover with a clean dishtowel until you are ready to use. Do not refrigerate.

HIP TIP: *You healthy types might like to try brown sushi rice—check for it at the market!*

FREE-FOR-ALL, MAKE-AND-SHARE SUSHI

This dinner party happens in the kitchen, where everyone can participate. Here's everything you'll need to pull it off.

ESSENTIALS

Bamboo mats	6 mats
Nori (toasted seaweed)	a large pack of 30 sheets (cut in half for smaller rolls)
Cooked sushi rice	10 cups (recipe on previous page)
Finger bowls of water	to keep rice from sticking to hands
A good serrated knife	for cutting rolls
A sharp kitchen knife	for cutting fish
Plastic wrap	for inside-out rolls
Clean towels	to keep hands and surfaces clean
Cutting boards	for cutting fish and rolls
Small bowls	for soy sauce, wasabi, and pickled ginger
Chopsticks	as utensils

FISH: CHEF'S CHOICE

Super fresh sushi-grade fish—usually sold in Asian markets in small packages, so you can buy small amounts and have variety at your party. Choose no more than half a pound each from the following list:

Tuna	ahi, albacore, yellowtail, and ground tuna are all fun to try
Salmon	
Snapper	
Sea Bass	
Scallops	
Eel	this is found already cooked, usually in a barbecue sauce
Orange tobiko (fish roe)	1/2 cup
Tobiko wasabi	1/2 cup, this roe is soaked in wasabi and bright green

ACCOMPANIMENTS

Japanese cucumber	2, seeded and cut into thin strips
Scallions	1 bunch, some sliced, others cut into strips
Carrot	1, peeled and julienned
Red bell pepper	1, thinly sliced
Mango	1, peeled, pitted, and thinly sliced
Avocado	3, peeled, pitted, and sliced into wedges
Red cabbage	1 or 2 leaves, shredded (to give color to the rolls)
Radish sprouts	1 bunch, trimmed of roots
Hearts of palm	1 (14-ounce) jar, drained (cut larger hearts in half lengthwise)

CONDIMENTS

Soy sauce or tamari
Wasabi
Pickled ginger
Japanese chili flake powder
Mayonnaise

. . . .

HIP TIP: Make vegetarians feel welcome by offering tasty fish substitutes for their rolls. Hearts of palm (found in a jar at most grocery stores) have a texture and briny flavor that imitates seafood wonderfully. Folded scrambled egg (tamago) or tofu is also yummy.

SPICY TUNA ROLLS

A universal favorite, this maki-roll filling requires a little bit of prep. Some people like mayonnaise—others don't. Be a Hip-host and make two versions! If you love preparing fillings like this one, why not combine scallops with mango and orange roe, or barbecued eel with smashed avocado, scallions, and sesame seeds?

Ground tuna	1/2 pound (or dice ahi tuna into ¼ inch cubes)
Sesame oil	1/2 teaspoon
Soy sauce	1 teaspoon
Chili oil	a few shakes of the bottle
Japanese chili flake powder	a few shakes of the bottle
Scallions	1–2, finely chopped (about 1 tablespoon)
Toasted white sesame seeds	1/2 teaspoon
Black sesame seeds	1/2 teaspoon
Wasabi mayonnaise	1 teaspoon, optional (use store-bought or make your own by adding wasabi to mayonnaise)

Combine all the ingredients. Taste, and adjust the seasoning to your taste buds' desire.

1. Lay the bamboo mat on a flat surface with the strips horizontal to you. Place a sheet of nori on the mat. Have a bowl of water nearby.

2. Dip your fingertips into the water, so the rice doesn't stick when you grab it. Spread a thin layer of rice, half a cup or so, onto the entire surface of the nori. Be stingy with the rice—you don't want too much. (For an inside-out roll, place a sheet of plastic wrap over the rice layer, and flip. Place the sheet plastic-side down on the rolling mat, and lay out another very thin layer of rice on the other side of the nori. Proceed as below.)

3. Now comes the fun part—compose your roll! Fill the bottom third of your roll with whatever your heart desires. Choose one type of fish. Accompaniments should complement the fish and give color and texture to the rolls. A spicy tuna roll may need no other ingredients, while an eel roll might love a few bell pepper slices, cucumber, and mango. Be an experimental artist. Some rolls will be thin, others fat. Everything will look great once you've plated it!

4. Place your fingers on the ingredients, and bring the bottom end of the rolling mat over the ingredients. We call this the "fold-over." Continue rolling! Let your fingers do the walking—exert a firm but gentle pressure for a nice, tight roll. (For the inside-out roll, remove the plastic wrap as you roll the mat, and then wrap it around the roll.)

5. Gently squeeze the mat around the roll until it's firm and even. Sometimes, we like to roll in the shape of a triangle, or even a square. Try it, once you've become confident in the process! (For the inside-out roll, now decorate the rice on the outside of your roll with sesame seeds and/or fish roe.)

6. Place the roll on a cutting board. Using a serrated knife, cut the roll into two equal portions. From there, cut it into sixths or eigths, whichever you prefer.

7. Contemplatively arrange the cut sushi on a plate, and decorate with veggies, sesame seeds, roe, dynamite sauce—whatever simple touches your magnificent roll calls for, to highlight its flavor and beauty.

✂ HIP TIP: *As your pals are having the time of their lives becoming expert sushi chefs, give them a caterpillar-roll challenge: Prepare an inside-out roll with different veggies in the center. Cut and adorn the top with slices of sashimi-ed tuna, salmon, bass, snapper, etc. Don't forget the radish sprout antenna!*

MATCHA TEACAKES

End your meal with a flourish and serve these sweet little cakes—they're not too sweet and are delightfully green.

Butter	*1/2 stick*
Sugar	*1/2 cup*
Eggs	*2, separated*
Unbleached flour	*1 cup*
Matcha	*1½ teaspoons (premium green tea powder)*
Baking powder	*1 teaspoon*
Nori	*1 sheet for decorating (if you're feeling artsy)*

Preheat oven to 325°F.

Cream the butter and sugar with an electric mixer until light and fluffy, scraping the bowl to incorporate the ingredients. Add the egg yolks and mix until combined.

Whip the egg whites until stiff, and fold into the butter mixture.

Next, combine the flour, matcha, and baking powder. Inhale the green tea flavor. Gently stir into the egg mixture. The batter will be quite thick. Don't worry!

Fill a greased muffin pan with the batter about halfway up the sides and decorate the tops with cut pieces of nori. At Hipcooks, we like to use a silicone mini-muffin pan, so that we get cute little cakes that pop right out of the pan.

Bake for about 25 minutes until set. Serve with a dusting of powdered sugar, or in solitary splendor.

. . . .

HIP TIP: *No time to bake for your sushi-making extravaganza? Store-bought mochi are also delicious: try green tea, mango, or chocolate.*

MAKE-AHEAD NOTES

For you trip-planning types....here are some make-ahead lists for each menu. For those who prefer to wing it, just grab your bootstraps and *enjoy the journey!*

2 days before	1 day before	the day of	upon serving
RAGIN' CAJUN			
marinate the chicken for the gumbo	make the gumbo while dancin' to jazz, blues, and zydeco	pop in the cornbread	heat up that gumbo, now
buy the beer and chill (you and the beer)		assemble turnips and greens	make Bananas Foster
JAMAICAN ME CRAZY			
soak the dried beans	make the jerk and marinate the chicken	make the black bean salad	reheat the callaloo
make the tea and sample the cocktail	make the callaloo	prepare ingredients for the shrimp and papaya salad	grill the chicken
	cook the black beans	sample the cocktail again	grill the pineapple
	make the ice cream and soak the pineapple in rum		
HOLY MOLE!			
roast the tomatoes	make the salsa	assemble the chile rellenos	make margaritas
toast and soak the chiles	make the mole	make the flan	bake the chicken and reheat the mole
THE THRILL OF THE GRILL			
make the mousse as you tango around the kitchen	grill the zucchini for the parcels	assemble the zucchini parcels	open the malbec
	cook the mushrooms	make the chimichurri	grill the steaks
	make the clerico		sit back and relax
A NIGHT IN CASABLANCA			
marinate the chicken	make the tagine	poach the apricots and make the filling	bake the b'stilla
make the b'stilla filling	soak the apricots	make the parsley salad	warm the tagine
		assemble the b'stilla	make the couscous
¡VIVA ESPAÑA!			
marinate the squid	prep the sofrito ingredients for the paella	make the bruschetta	sear the squid
make the red wine soaked citrus		choose a delicious rioja	clap your hands, stamp your feet, and make the paella

2 days before	1 day before	the day of	upon serving

LA BELLE ÉPOQUE

2 days before	1 day before	the day of	upon serving
marinate the beef for the bourguignon	make the beef bourguignon minus the finishing touches	open the oysters and make the leek sauce	warm the leek sauce and poach the oysters
	assemble the tarte tatin	make and add the finishing touches to the beef	warm the bourguignon and make the accompaniment
	decide what accompaniment you'd like for the beef bourguignon	marvel at your cooking prowess	bake the tarte tatin and make the glacée

MY BIG FAT GREEK DINNER PARTY

2 days before	1 day before	the day of	upon serving
assemble the spanikopita and freeze (well-covered)	grill the veggies	make the tzatziki	sauté the halloumi and serve with ouzo
make the baklava	marinate the lamb	make the veggie salad	bake the spanikopita
		set the table with non-breakable plates	cook the lamb

1001 ARABIAN NIGHTS

2 days before	1 day before	the day of	upon serving
make the crème brûlée and chill, covered	assemble the meatballs	make the khoresht fesenjaan or assemble the components of the shirin-polow	sear the meatballs and serve with accompaniments
decide to make the khoresht fesenjaan or the shirin-polow (or both)	make the maast-o khiar	decorate with candles everywhere	reheat the khoresht fesenjaan or finish the shirin-polow
			torch the brûlée

SHORTCUT TO NIRVANA

2 days before	1 day before	the day of	upon serving
make the mango chutney, green sauce, and raita	make the chicken tikka masala	make the fancy basmati rice and keep on the back of the stove so that it stays warm	poof the papadums and serve with the three sauces
marinate the chicken	watch a Bollywood movie	make the saag paneer	reheat the chicken and the saag
			make the sorbet

THAI ONE ON

2 days before	1 day before	the day of	upon serving
decide on the green or the red curry	make either the green or the red curry dish	make the spring rolls and declare your love of fish sauce	steam and finish the coconut sticky rice
crack open a Singha and get cracking on the curry paste	soak white and forbidden rice		reheat the curry
			steam and assemble the forbidden rice

TURNING JAPANESE

2 days before	1 day before	the day of	upon serving
chill the sake and take it easy	sample a saketini to make sure it's just as good as it sounds	make the sushi rice	get all your veggies ready
		make the teacakes	slice the fish
	shop for fish	assemble the inari skins	make the spicy tuna

INDEX

What Hipcooks students have to say about our classes:

You've given me confidence in the kitchen!

Last night was my first time at Hipcooks and I have to say...I am hooked.

Now I use my taste buds more than my teaspoons.

Hipcooks is as fresh as the ingredients you use.

I can see this becoming a wonderful habit.

I think Hipcooks could take over the world

Bigger than McDonald's!

Hipcooks East Los Angeles
642 Moulton Ave Unit E21
Los Angeles, CA 90031
hipcooks@hipcooks.com

Hipcooks West Los Angeles
2833 S Robertson Blvd
Los Angeles, CA 90034
hipcooks@hipcooks.com

Hipcooks San Diego
4048 30th Street
San Diego, CA 92104
sd@hipcooks.com

We learned so much and your recipes are incredible! We were literally giggling the whole way home.

I've said my whole life that "I can't cook." Now I've hosted two fabulous dinner parties and I use a few of the recipes on a regular basis.

Your concept and approach really resonated with me...I have been cooking up a storm!

We loved making the food as much as eating it.

Yum
Yum
Yum!

Hipcooks Portland
3808 N Williams
Suite 120
Portland, OR 97227
pdx@hipcooks.com

Hipcooks Seattle
217 Yale Ave North
Seattle, WA 98109
seattle@hipcooks.com

Hipcooks Orange County
125 N Broadway
Suite C
Santa Ana, CA 92701
oc@hipcooks.com

THANK YOU to my family—
Lucia Reti Meadows, the littelest
Hipcook. DANKE to **Erika Reti**
and GRACIAS to **Aldo Reti**, for
allowing me to grow up with such
wonderful food. CHEERS to
my family all around the globe
(the Brazilian **Retis**, my Argentine
cousins, the Italian Contingent, my
beautiful Iranian cousins, and my
family in the US) for putting me up
on many a couch. I look forward
to reciprocating with all of your
children!

Kisses to **Andie**, for being the most
wonderful sister and happy eater,
and for good times cleaning the
kitchen floor by skating on sponges.

MERCI Hipcooks Managers **Kyrsten Beidelman**
for her editing and endless energy and **Bonny Giardina**
for cooking it up with me at the cookbook shoot.
So much love to all the Hipcooks crew—you rock
it! Hipcooks LA: **Alyson Teijeira**, **Angela Turrou**,
Erika Green, **Jennie O'Connor**, **Jessie Wan**, **Joy Jansen**,
Kyrsten Beidelman, **Lisa Posas**, and **Selene Zander**.
Hipcooks Portland: **Cheyenne Terbrueggen**, **Peter
Calley**, **Melanie Boekee**, and **Suzana Pinkerton**.
Hipcooks Seattle: **Bonny Giardina**. Hipcooks San Diego:
Tristan Blash. Here's a "Hear, hear!" to all the
fabulous Hipcooks TAs.

TANK YU **Dave Zobel**. this project would not have
existed without your enthusiasm. You da best!

GRACIAS **Lissa Hahn**, the most
talented photographer, fabulous prop stylist, amazing
creative director, stress-manager, and all-around
good friend. I can't wait to create the next cookbook
with you! Thanks also for creative input from
Chris McClary, **Lauren Hurley**, and **Olivia Dunn**.

ARIGATO **Pam Zsorsi** from Ink and
Peat for graciously lending last-minute
props! Thank you also to **Claire Dugoni,
Diedre Smith, Holly Krass-Bell, Kathleen
Kranenburg**, and **Mini Sharma Ogle** for
props. Props to you!

Efharistó Fundraising campaign supporters: Bev Alzedo, Joy Jansen, Erika Reti, David & Ginni Spencer, Sandy Brasseale, Kira Reed Lorsch, Andrew, Bonnie Heckler, Lynne & Bryan Volk, Carol Waldo, Eli Snell, Gillian Chessé, Giovanni Arcadu, Richard Norman, Sarah Hale, Sarah McKaig, Tara & Annginette, Allison DeHaan, Andrew & Mary Lim, Anthony R Holy, Barbara Mutnick, Bonnie Lowrance, Carol Ann Timmel-witschi, Caroline Barlow, Colleen Henson, Constance Lively, Cori Roed, Craig Minami, Dirk-Jan and Melanie Boekee, Drew Fleischer, Elizabeth Warren, Erika and Matt, Frank H. McLaughlin, Heather Adams, Holly Menoher, Jaime Green, Jamie Loeb Schmale, Jane Vaden, Jessie Wan, Liz Argall, Louise Hamlin, Meghan Robertson, Michele Francisco, Michelle Vering, Mr. & Mrs. Irfan and Leslie Khan, Rhonda Anisman, Sharene Kuhrt, Spirit Creek Catering, Stephanie R. Cass, Terry Buchholz, The Boulin family, Valarie Grudier Edwards, and William Archer.

And last but not least, eternal gratitude to my mentor, cheerleader, and silent partner HW.

Visas

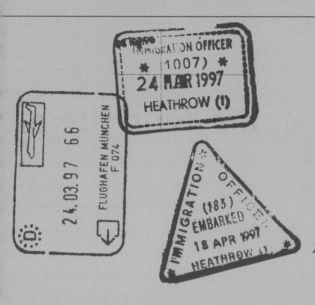

IMMIGRATION OFFICER
* (1007) *
24 MAR 1997
HEATHROW (1)

24.03.97 66
FLUGHAFEN MÜNCHEN
F 074

IMMIGRATION OFFICER
(183)
EMBARKED
18 APR 1997
HEATHROW (1)

VALID FOR 90 DAYS RENEWABLE
FOR THE SAME PERIOD BY THE
FEDERAL POLICE. TOTAL STAY 180
DAYS A YEAR.

ATÉ 180 DIAS POR ANO.

REPÚBLICA FEDERATIVA DO BRASIL

A 0776050

Grátis
VISTO TURISTA
Nº 1280
Nome
Name   Monika Reta

Válido por
Validity   Saida após entrada

Data de expedição
Issued on   8.07.96

Repartição expedidora
Issued by   CONSULADO GERAL DO
BRASIL EM MONTEVIDEO

Múltiplas entradas
Multiple entry(ies)

Assinatura
Signature

Passport number
Nº do passaporte   062974414

Raul E. A. d'E. Taunay
Cônsul Geral Adjunto

FIRST ENTRY WITHIN 90 DAYS
PRIMEIRA ENTRADA EM 90 DIAS

REPUBLICA DE VENEZUELA
Ministerio de Hacienda

Nombre del Solicitante

Número de Identificación   Fecha

Concepto   Base Legal

H-93   1551738

500 QUINIENTOS BOLIVARES

1.000 MIL BOLIVARES

5.000 CINCO MIL BOLIVARES

5.000 CINCO MIL BOLIVARES

5.000 CINCO MIL BOLIVARES

5.000 CINCO MIL BOLIVARES

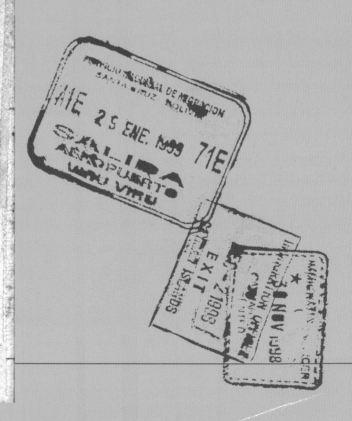

POLICIA NACIONAL DE MIGRACION
SANTA CRUZ BOLIVIA
AIE 25 ENE 1999 71E
SALIDA
AEROPUERTO